I0090617

ICNC **MONOGRAPH** SERIES

SERIES EDITOR: Maciej Bartkowski
VOLUME EDITOR: Amber French
EDITOR OF REVISED EDITION: Julia Constantine

Other volumes in this series:

Making or Breaking Nonviolent Discipline in Civil Resistance Movements, Jonathan Pinckney (2016)

The Power of Staying Put: Nonviolent Resistance against Armed Groups in Colombia, Juan Masullo (2015)

The Tibetan Nonviolent Struggle: A Strategic and Historical Analysis, Tenzin Dorjee (2015)

Published by ICNC Press
International Center on Nonviolent Conflict
1775 Pennsylvania Ave. NW, Suite 1200
Washington, D.C. 20006 USA

Revised Edition, July 2019
ISBN: 978-1-943271-10-8

Cover photos: June 2015, Plaza de la Constitucion (Constitution Plaza), Guatemala City, Guatemala. Findings of the CICIG, the post-war anti-impunity international council, triggered mass mobilization against government corruption and impunity, leading to the resignation and arrest of President Otto Perez and Vice President Roxana Baldetti. Photos courtesy of Tomas Ayuso.

Peer Review: This ICNC monograph underwent blind peer review to be considered for publication. Scholarly experts in the field of civil resistance and related disciplines, as well as practitioners of nonviolent actions, serve as independent reviewers of the ICNC monograph manuscripts.

Publication Disclaimer: The designations used and material presented in this publication do not indicate the expression of any opinion whatsoever on the part of ICNC. The author holds responsibility for the selection and presentation of facts contained in this work, as well as for any and all opinions expressed therein, which are not necessarily those of ICNC and do not commit the organization in any way.

People Power Movements and International Human Rights

CREATING A LEGAL FRAMEWORK

Summary

International human rights came into existence bottom-up, from the efforts of ordinary people to ally with each other in solidarity and demand their rights through civil resistance campaigns in support of democracy, an end to slavery and child labor, women's rights, labor rights, and tenant rights, among other rights. Yet international law recognizes only states as the ultimate source of law. This monograph develops a novel, people-powered or "*demos*-centric" approach to international human rights law that acknowledges the role in lawmaking of average human beings, seeing them as both the source of rights and the most effective means of overcoming the central weakness of international law—namely, its inability to ensure that states and governments comply with the human rights obligations they supposedly undertake. Taking account of nonviolent movements and their impact on the formation and implementation of international human rights law recognizes the human agency of the supposed beneficiaries of human rights law: common people.[1]

The monograph develops this approach using the controversial third source of law identified in Article 38 of the Statute of the International Court of Justice, namely, general principles. As a source of law, general principles are controversial because of their theological, natural law overtones. This monograph uses nonviolent civil resistance as a means of objectifying natural law and making it usable for a secular, inclusive and multicultural international legal system. Instead of an absolute term—something that exists eternally, independent of the mind of human beings—we can see natural law as a relative term that reflects a human, creative envisioning of an alternative legal order that is not yet reflected in positive legal codes but is being created intersubjectively through the collective work of human beings engaged in nonviolent civil resistance.

The analytical framework developed in this monograph identifies four general principles that structure the human rights project: nonexploitation, nondiscrimination, nonrepression and nonviolence. These general principles crosscut four dimensions of law (international and domestic law, positive and natural law) and comprise a human rights *ethos*. Using a typology derived from these four principles, nonviolent civil resistance movements may be critically examined for how fully they manifest this human rights *ethos*.

The monograph thus creates an interdisciplinary research agenda for future collaboration between legal scholars and social scientists while also making a contribution to the practice of civil resistance. Scholars of civil resistance studies can be attentive to evidence that the nonviolent movements they study are manifesting a human rights *ethos*. Legal scholars can evaluate this evidence and incorporate it as they develop and strengthen general principles of human rights law, in order to ensure conceptual consistency across the aforementioned four dimensions of law. Doing so will enable them to recognize the potential of nonviolent civil resistance movements to aid in the internalization of international law into domestic legal systems. Finally, practitioners of civil resistance, although primarily using extra-legal means, can become more strategic in their reliance on human rights instruments and treaties as well as general principles in waging more effective nonviolent struggles with better chances to uphold and broaden human rights norms and successfully redress injustices, including in repressive regimes.

Acknowledgments

Chosen through a blind, peer-reviewed competition, portions of this monograph were presented at the American Society of International Law's mid-year Research Forum in 2015 and a full draft was presented there in 2016. I am particularly grateful for detailed commentary from 2016 panel moderator Harlan Cohen. During the publication process, the monograph benefited greatly from feedback from editor Maciej Bartkowski, peer reviewer Mary Elizabeth King, and from an anonymous peer reviewer. The monograph was launched at the Atlantic Council in Washington, DC, in January 2018. I'd like to thank Maria J. Stephan and Sean Murphy for their insightful commentary and Mathew Burrows for his support. Outstanding research assistance was provided by Yisel Valdes and Alyssa Conn. Finally, thanks to Peter Ackerman for his generous support.

Table of Contents

LIST OF ACRONYMS

ANC	African National Congress
BCM	Black Consciousness Movement
CEDAW	Convention on the Elimination of All Forms of Discrimination Against Women
CICIG	International Commission Against Impunity in Guatemala
CSO	Civil Society Organization
DHRD	Declaration on Human Rights Defenders
ECtHR	European Court of Human Rights
FCPA	Foreign Corrupt Practices Act (US law)
FOIA	Freedom of Information Act
HRC	Human Rights Committee
IACHR	Inter-American Commission on Human Rights
IACtHR	Inter-American Court of Human Rights
ICC	International Criminal Court
ICCPR	International Covenant on Civil and Political Rights
ICESCR	International Covenant on Social, Economic, and Cultural Rights
ICJ	International Court of Justice
ILO	International Labor Organization
MKSS	Mazdoor Kisan Shakti Sangathan
NAVCO	Nonviolent and Violent Campaigns and Outcomes Dataset
NGO	Nongovernmental Organization
R2P	Responsibility to Protect
TWAIL	Third World Alternatives to International Law
UDF	United Democratic Front
UDHR	Universal Declaration of Human Rights
UN	United Nations
UNCAC	United Nations Convention Against Corruption
UNECOSOC	United Nations Economic and Social Council
UNGA	United Nations General Assembly
UN GA Res.	United Nations General Assembly Resolution
UN HR Res.	United Nations Human Rights Council Resolution
UNHRC	United Nations Human Rights Council
UPR	United Nations Universal Periodic Review

Introduction

*T*he masses of people are rising up. And wherever they are assembled today, whether they are in Johannesburg, South Africa; Nairobi, Kenya; Accra, Ghana; New York City; Atlanta, Georgia; Jackson, Mississippi; or Memphis, Tennessee, the cry is always the same — "We want to be free."[2]

"What do you want to tell Assad?" "I am a human being." "I am free." "I want justice."[3]

This monograph creates a framework to situate nonviolent civil resistance or "people power" movements in the context of international human rights law. In so doing, it builds a bridge between two academic disciplines that currently stand as worlds apart, with little cross-over or cross-fertilization: human rights law and nonviolent civil resistance studies. Often confused with "passive resistance" or "pacifism," nonviolent civil resistance is a civilian-based method used to wage conflict through social, psychological, economic, and political means without the threat or use of force. It includes acts of omission, acts of commission, or a combination of both. Most practitioners of civil resistance see themselves as operating outside the law. At the same time, international human rights law takes little account of civil resistance movements, which are without formal legal status, though certain human rights norms apply to them as well as to individuals.

The international legal community is, however, beginning to take notice of civil resistance, at least to the extent of defining the scope of a right to peaceful protest. This monograph will focus on human rights law as the part of international law most relevant to nonviolent movements, but more general aspects of international law are implicated as well.

International human rights jurists and scholars have reason to give nonviolent civil resistance increased attention. Civil resistance movements are occurring with increasing frequency all over the world. A study by the Carnegie Endowment for International Peace finds that "major citizen protests are multiplying,"[6] many of them part of coordinated civil resistance campaigns. After an earlier phase of increased activity in the late 1980s and early 1990s ended, the pace of such protests picked up again in 2005 and "have reached a new peak in the past five years."[7] Since 2010, more than 60 countries have experienced major protests. "Just in 2015, significant protests took place in Armenia, Azerbaijan, Bosnia, Brazil, Burundi, the Democratic Republic of Congo, Guatemala, Iraq, Japan, Lebanon, Macedonia, Malaysia, Moldova, and Venezuela. The list of countries hit by major protests since 2010 is remarkably long and diverse."[8] An idea of the explosive growth of civil resistance movements is illustrated by the following chart:

Onsets of New Nonviolent Campaigns, 1900-2015

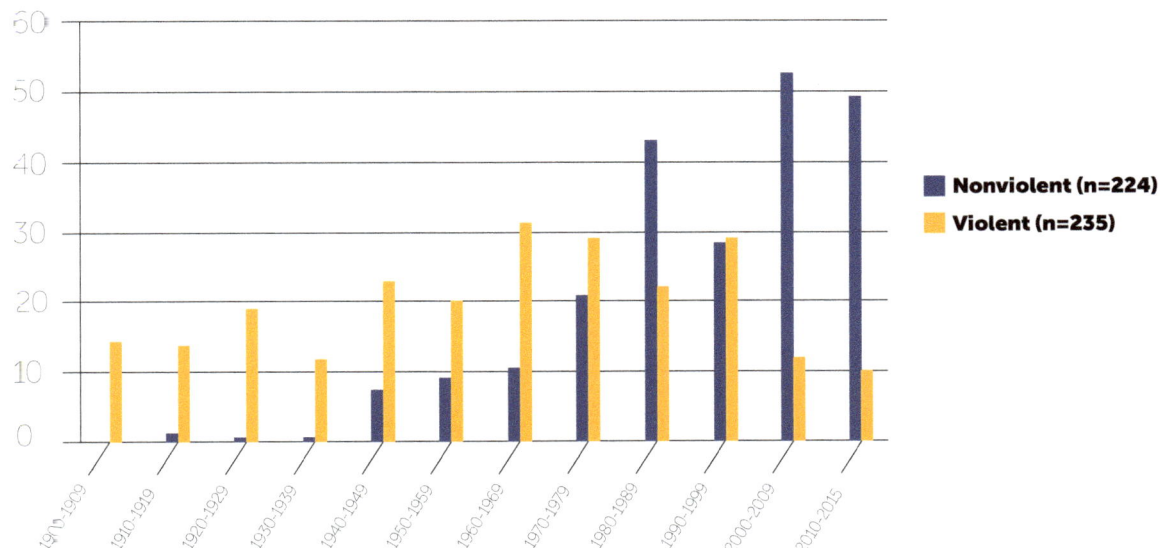

Source: Erica Chenoweth and Maria J. Stephan, "How the World is Proving Martin Luther King Right about Nonviolence", *Washington Post*, January 18, 2016. https://www.washingtonpost.com/news/monkey-cage/wp/2016/01/18/how-the-world-is-proving-mlk-right-about-nonviolence/

In fact, this graph provides at best a partial picture because it only shows large-scale civil resistance movements, where the goals are revolutionary or "maximalist": "to remove the incumbent national leadership from power or to create territorial independence through secession or expulsion of a foreign military occupation or colonial power."[9] The wave of global protest seen since 2005 has been compared to a similar wave occurring in the 1980s and 1990s, except that in contrast to earlier waves, today's protests are occurring in every region of the world and in countries with every type of governmental regime.[10] It has been said that "nonviolent resistance campaigns have become the modal category of contentious action worldwide."[11]

Not only are nonviolent movements becoming more frequent, they have over time demonstrated their ability to have potent effects on international relations worldwide, altering the geopolitical order in ways long considered the prerogative of states. In Central and Eastern Europe, nonviolent movements helped to bring about the fall of the Soviet Union. Nonviolent civil resistance helped many nations win independence or end colonialism (United States, Egypt, India, Ghana, Malawi, and East Timor, to name a few).[12] The Cedar Revolution drove Syrian forces out of Lebanon in 2005.

Civil resistance movements have also changed the nature of the international community and, by extension, international law through their ability to affect major political changes in the internal governance of member states. Throughout history, people power movements have successfully and tangibly affected the specific nature and type of a state's government, either forcing political reforms, reshaping political institutions or transforming entire political systems. In many other countries besides the ones mentioned above, military juntas and other dictatorships have been overthrown, altering the balance between democratic and non-democratic states in the international order.

Though, technically, under international law, the nature of a state's government is a purely domestic matter; a state can only make international law through the actions (or omissions) of its government. Thus, as a practical matter, it makes a difference whether a state is democratic or undemocratic, welfarist or not, isolationist or interventionist, as its actions affects the formation of future conventional and customary international law.

Research into nonviolent civil resistance challenges the conventional wisdom that only violence "works." Quantitative analysis by Erica Chenoweth and Maria J. Stephan compared the effectiveness of 323 violent and nonviolent campaigns occurring between 1900 and 2006 and reached the startling conclusion that nonviolent campaigns achieved their objectives at over twice the rate of violent campaigns (53% of the time for nonviolent campaigns versus 26% for violent campaigns).[13] Chenoweth and Stephan conclude that this greater rate of success is owing to the greater ability of nonviolent movements to attract broad participation.[14] Because the "barriers to participation" are lower, nonviolent movements are typically much more inclusive than violent movements, including more women, elderly people, and youths.[15] While some may erroneously claim that nonviolent resistance only works against opponents unwilling to use harsh repression, in fact "[t]he vast majority of nonviolent campaigns have emerged in authoritarian regimes... where even peaceful opposition against the government may have fatal consequences."[16]

Given the increasing frequency and potency of nonviolent civil resistance worldwide, it is important to clarify its place in international law. As nonviolent campaigns have grown more frequent, so too has repressive government response. The United Nations Human Rights Council (UNHRC) has expressed concern in various resolutions[17] about the increasing use of violent attacks against peaceful protesters around the world, as well as the increasing tendency of states to criminalize protest activity and prosecute protesters, and it is taking steps to clarify the relevant law. We now appear to have entered a phase of retrenchment where democratic gains that once seemed unstoppable are now being turned back. Support for nonviolent resistance may be crucial to pushing back against this turning tide.

While the international law that applies to civil resistance movements is being clarified, larger questions of how such movements relate to international human rights law have not been deeply addressed. This monograph creates a space for civil resistance movements in international law by identifying grassroots and bottom-up mechanisms for shaping and making international norms. In its essence, this monograph proposes a theory of nonviolent civil resistance in international law, showing how it can be developed and empirically understood as both a subject and a maker of international law.

The analysis undertaken in this monograph requires a rethinking of fundamental aspects of international human rights law, and international law more generally. Traditionally, international law does not accord lawmaking powers to individuals or other non-state actors.[18] Individuals have rights and some duties under international law, but they can only indirectly affect lawmaking (e.g., by influencing the diplomatic negotiations over international multilateral treaties) rather than be the originators of law themselves.[19] Similarly, as Balakrishnan Rajagopal notes, "Modern international law does not ordinarily concede mass movements and local struggles as makers of legal change."[20] To the extent that international law takes account of social movements, it is only in the context of self-determination and state formation, through the doctrine of "effective control." This doctrine holds that whichever government has "effective control" of a state's territory is recognized as a legitimate authority in the international system. Thus, even in this context, as Rajagopal further notes, "international law leaves the terrain as long as the situation is murky, and 'returns' only to welcome the victor to the club of states."[21] In short, international law takes no account of the actions of individuals or groups as lawmakers, except indirectly, through pressuring states to take action or proposing norms that states subsequently adopt.

The reason for this disregard of individuals and other non-state actors is owing to the state-centric nature of the international system, which remains largely reflective of the sovereign nation-state system created by the Peace of Westphalia in 1648.[22] In this system, political authority is centralized and territorial, not dispersed and personal as it was during the Middle Ages. The classic description of the concept of sovereignty created by the Peace of Westphalia was given by US Supreme Court Chief Justice John Marshall, who said, "The jurisdiction of the nation within its own territory is necessarily exclusive and absolute. It is susceptible of no limitation not imposed by itself."[23] The state-based system has been called anarchical because it lacks the central features of domestic law, namely, a central legislator or global police power. Stability in this anarchical international system has been long thought to rest on mutual respect for state sovereignty, as guaranteed by the corollary norms of equality among the states and nonintervention.

Because the international system lacks central features of domestic law, its underlying legal premise is *voluntarism*: the idea that states *consent* to participate in international law. As a consequence, state-centric international law is mainly "positivist," meaning that law is created through the practice of states. States either make explicit compacts with one another through treaties, or they evolve patterns of interaction (customs) that create predictable and stable international relations. Though no state functions as the supreme sovereign, states taken together are lawmakers, though occasionally they may delegate lawmaking power to international organizations. With a qualification discussed below, states, in the current international order, are the only entity with lawmaking power. As set out in Article 38 of the Statute of the International Court of Justice (ICJ), state-centric international law recognizes three "sources" of law, of which the first two are overwhelmingly more important:

1) international agreements or treaties (conventional law);
2) state practice undertaken with a sense of legal obligation (customary law);
3) "general principles of law recognized by civilized nations."

A fourth source of law, "judicial decisions and the teachings of the most highly qualified publicists of the various nations" may also be consulted "as subsidiary means" for determining rules of law."[24] Also considered by some scholars only a "subsidiary means," the third source of law, general principles is the only "source" of law that does not emanate exclusively from states, but until now, general principles have not been theorized as encompassing the practice of individuals.

While most approaches to international human rights law look at it only through the state-centric framework of traditional international law, this monograph takes a more deep-seated approach and examines how people power movements may be considered makers of international law. Traditional international law discounts the people as a source of law, vesting sovereignty (and thus lawmaking power) in the state alone. But as Mahatma Gandhi declared long ago, "[E]ven the most powerful cannot rule without the co-operation of the ruled."[25] The theory underlying nonviolent civil resistance as a political strategy rejects the conventional view that political power is monolithic and centralized in the head of state.[26] Even in the most authoritarian political regimes, power is multidimensional and depends on myriad "pillars of support,"[27] the human capital without which power cannot exert its control. The police and the military are the most obvious pillars of support, but power also depends on more intangible or indirect supports like the media and the business community. In every civil resistance campaign, the challenge for organizers is to analyze the pillars of support most relevant to the targeted regime and devise tactics to weaken their loyalty. As Srdja Popovic explains, "the nonviolent struggle is about pulling people from pillars. It is not about pushing and pressing and bringing down and bombing and destroying. It is about, can you persuade the people to step out?"[28] As the pillars of support fall away, the regime weakens and eventually collapses. The premise of this monograph—drawn from civil resistance studies—is that people power undergirds the state that is the lawmaker in international law.

Whatever the justification for refusing to recognize individuals as lawmakers in the context of other areas of international law, it is peculiarly wrongheaded when it comes to international human rights law.[29] If human rights are rights that people have by virtue of their humanness, which is the most basic and accepted (if mysterious) definition, then human rights are not *created* by either international or domestic law. At the same time, although not created by international or domestic law, human rights may be *protected* and *realized* by either or both. The rights in question are *human* rights, not *states* rights. They are for the benefit of *individuals*, not for the benefit of *states*.[30]

International human rights law did not come into existence top-down, out of the benevolent intentions of states, even though states eventually began to recognize that large-scale human rights abuses could pose a threat to the international order. Rather, it came into existence from the bottom-up efforts of ordinary people in civil society to ally with each other in solidarity and demand their rights, often through organized nonviolent campaigns and movements that pressured elites and powerholders to recognize individual rights (freedom for slaves, women's rights, labor rights, and children's rights, to name a few). Unlike international law generally, the real source of international human rights law has been the coordinated, organized and nonviolently forceful efforts of individuals—in other words, what one can refer to as people power.

But how to take account of this power when international law takes no account of the activities of "non-state actors," as human beings are antiseptically referred to in international law? Indeed, when it comes to sources of law, traditional international law generally does not even take account of domestic legal systems, except in so far as to consider domestic judicial decisions interpreting international law as secondary sources.[31] This monograph attempts to solve this central theoretical dilemma, and thus to start to forge what might be called a "people-centered" or *demos*-centric approach to international human rights law, by developing the third source of law called general principles and identifying four specific general principles that arguably define the modern human rights project. When respected by a nonviolent resistance movement, these four principles create a human rights *ethos*—a spirit or attitude animating and reflected in a practice—that can be said to characterize the movement. This people-centered approach will, in turn, allow us to recognize a more prominent role of organized human agency (e.g., in a form of civil resistance movements) in the shaping and making of international law.

This monograph is structured like a traditional legal analysis and divided into two halves. The first half determines the applicable law by setting out the relevant legal frameworks and then progressively develops them to take account of people power as expressed in organized nonviolent movements or campaigns. Titled "Theorizing People Power in International Law: General Principles of Human Rights," the first half of the monograph creates a new, multidimensional analytical framework for international human rights and explains its theoretical basis in law. The second half of the monograph, titled "Applying General Principles of Human Rights to Specific People Power Movements," takes that new analytical framework and concretely applies it in particular situations, unfolding it from one dimension of law—international, domestic, positive and natural—to the next. Though this is first and foremost a legal analysis, written by a lawyer from the perspective of legal practice and scholarship, this monograph will develop criteria for identifying when specific civil resistance movements may be said to manifest a human rights *ethos* and thus will identify a research agenda that social scientists can pursue going forward, perhaps in collaboration with legal scholars, in their work on civil resistance movements.

The Analytical Framework Derived:
Four Dimensions and Four Principles

Of the three traditional sources of law, the most undeveloped—general principles— is the most amenable to incorporating the practice of non-state actors, including civil resistance movements, as a source of law. Unlike treaties and custom, general principles do not depend on state practice for their validity, though they need to be objectifiable in some fashion. They have been called "the most controversial of the various sources of international law enumerated in Article 38 of the Statute and thus of international law in general."[32] For the purposes of this monograph, what is significant about general principles as a source of law is that they are a hybrid form of law, potentially operating in four dimensions across both international and domestic law, and both positive and natural law.

While the particular language of Article 38 ("general principles of law recognized by all civilized nations") was a compromise negotiated during the drafting process between those advocating for a natural law approach and those insisting that general principles derive only from domestic law (*in foro domestico*),[33] over time the latter aspect of general principles has come to dominate. Used to fill gaps in international law through reference to domestic legal systems, general principles are mainly seen in the legal literature as a conduit through which doctrines from national legal systems travel up into international law. This aspect makes them a natural source for human rights law, which operates at the interface of domestic and international law. In addition to being a conduit for domestic law, general principles can potentially encompass natural law as well, though this aspect is far more controversial than their domestic law aspect and is almost wholly undeveloped doctrinally. The natural law provenance of general principles has been most evident in the jurisprudence of international tribunals.[34] However, when general principles are described as having a "natural law flavor"[35] or "overtone," this is generally not meant to be a compliment. Perhaps the most positive appraisal is Henkin's remark that general principles represent "the triumph of good sense and practical needs" over the constraints and limitations imposed as a result of a purely positive-law, state-centric approach to international law.[36]

It is not hard to understand why the natural law provenance of general principles has not been celebrated or developed doctrinally. Today's international law grew out of an earlier view of international order called the law of nations. When the law of nations was first theorized by the great jurists like Hugo Grotius and Emmerich de Vattel in the 17th and 18th centuries, states were also thought to be subject to natural law, which was believed to originate in the mind of God or in human nature, and was binding on states as moral "persons." Over time, natural law, and its close cousin natural rights, fell into disfavor, as legal positivism, with its emphasis on "positive law" or "man-made" law, emerged and was embraced by most Western legal traditions starting from the mid- to late-19th century. Natural law was rejected, either because it was seen to be subjective or resting on a theological framework. But during the years when natural law was seen as a source of law, the law of nations was considered to rest not just on the consent of states but on the consent of all mankind. For instance, Blackstone noted that "[t]he law of nations is a system of rules... established by the universal consent among civilized inhabitants of the world" and "all the people."[37] In 1796, US Supreme Court Justice Samuel Chase pronounced that the customary law of nations is "established by the general consent of mankind."[38]

This monograph uses people power to recuperate the natural law aspect of general principles and takes the additional step of arguing that a vague term like the "conscience of mankind" can be objectified by looking at people power as its enactment when people harness their power. Ever since Antigone defied the edicts of Creon, King of Thebes, in order to secure her brother a proper burial, disobedience of positive law in the name of a higher justice has been recognized as a justifiable transgression.[39] The justice Antigone pursued was not the law of the land, but its content was clear and so were the actions that she took based upon it—covering her brother's body with earth and reciting burial rites—actions for which she was condemned to death.

To develop an approach to people power as natural law, it will be helpful to turn to the work of the legal scholar Robert Cover, who theorized law as not just created by courts but socially created by people.[40] Cover used the term *jurisgenesis* to refer to "the creation of legal meaning" by the *nomos*, or normative universe, of different social groups within a society,[41] a process of meaning-creation that takes place through culture.[42] As Cover remarks, "No set of legal institutions or prescriptions exists apart from the narratives that locate it and give it meaning."[43]

People power can thus help us conceptualize natural law in a new way that makes it more concrete and independent of a theological, or any eternal, foundation, and thus more usable as a source of law. Instead of an absolute term—something that exists eternally, independent of the mind of human beings—we can see natural law as a relative term that reflects a new world being imagined through the creative efforts of individuals engaged in the collective social activity of nonviolent resistance. Where there is no law, or only bad law, human rights defenders will have recourse to the tools of natural rights—civil disobedience, noncooperation, boycotts, stay-a-ways and so on. Before human rights were positive law, they were imagined natural rights—moral or political ideals that motivated social movements: for example, abolition, the fight for women's suffrage and equal rights, labor organizing, the movement to end child labor, and campaigns for indigenous people's rights. Moral ideals became positive rights through the different phases of *jurisgenesis* and were propelled by activism of regular people demanding these rights. "Abolitionism was a social movement that had as its goal a change in society," legal scholar Jenny Martinez observes, "But the change abolitionists sought was also fundamentally a change in law: slavery and slave-trading were legal, and the abolitionists wanted them to be illegal."[44]

But whereas Cover's idea of *jurisgenesis* was unbounded, available to all social groups, this monograph undertakes to delineate the contours of *jurisgenesis* directed specifically to the realization of human rights. To do this, it is necessary to discover the narrative driving the genesis of legal meaning in relation to international human rights law. This monograph will define the human rights project as a legal-moral cultural process aimed at creating and realizing a *nomos* or normative universe that is characterized by a particular human rights *ethos*. This *ethos* consists of different iterations of a basic narrative, in which the social *teloi*, or ends, of freedom, justice, and peace are imagined to be achievable through specific means. These means encompass the realization of human dignity through individual and collective activity organized around four general principles of nondiscrimination, nonrepression, nonexploitation, and nonviolence.[45]

The Analytical Framework Applied

The second half of the monograph applies this analytical framework to four broad types of real-world scenarios involving civil resistance movements and shows how the general principles outlined above operate across the four dimensions of international and domestic, positive and natural law. The first scenario looks at how human rights law may be used to protect participants in nonviolent movements. The second scenario illustrates how people power movements may invoke, appeal to, or organize themselves in relation to positive human rights law, even to the extent of being an adjunct to legal implementation. The third scenario creates a matrix for assessing when movements that assert rights outside of the framework of positive human rights law can be considered as manifesting a human rights *ethos*. The fourth scenario returns the analysis to positive law and proposes three ways, in relation to three substantive areas of law, that civil resistance movements can be looked at as contributing to the development of general principles as a source of international human rights law and can thus be seen as making international law.

Addressing a Potential Criticism

A line of critique, mainly coming from scholars from the "Third World," particularly scholars associated with the TWAIL network, or "Third World Alternatives to International Law,"[46] claims that the human rights project is fatally biased by its Western origins and priorities. Rather than seeing the attempt that this monograph makes to extend the framework of human rights law to grassroots and popular movements as a good thing, this line of critique might observe that such analysis embraces the hegemonic approach of Western legal language and practice and thereby edges out more indigenous "languages of emancipation" that have different "epistemological foundations," in the words of Rajogopal.[47] As such, this approach leads "to the construction of new global orthodoxies through programs to export US legal institutions and expertise."[48] There are two possible responses to this criticism.

The first response is that this critique is founded heavily on the claim that the human rights project privileges Western civil and political rights and marginalizes social and economic rights, the latter of which are often of greater concern to Third

World constituencies. While this claim is not without grounds, especially as a historical matter, the fact is that social and economic rights were incorporated into the Universal Declaration of Human Rights (UDHR), the central legal document at the foundation of international human rights law. In addition, they are increasingly being incorporated on an equal footing in binding human rights legal frameworks. To the extent that human rights obligations have been tied to neoliberal structural adjustment policies having deleterious domestic effects on developing nations, the problem lies not with the human rights norms *per se* but with those economic policies.

The second response is to realize, as Rajagopal a few years later conceded, that human rights is a language "of both power and resistance... of hegemony and counter-hegemony"[49] and thus "a terrain of contestation."[50] If local movements do not wish to avail themselves of coordinating with international human rights legal frameworks, they are free not to. But human rights have a high degree of legitimacy, both among elites and general populations. Sensing the importance of that legitimacy, grassroots movements across different geographies, cultures, and political systems often implicitly or explicitly avail themselves of human rights practice and discourse in their organizing and resistance practices. Therefore, the aim of the monograph is to set out the means and possible advantages of creating greater synergies between civil resistance movements and formal legal frameworks.

Readers who are not legal specialists will benefit from first reviewing the main terms and concepts that this monograph employs and are encouraged to refer back to them while going through the monograph. A glossary of terms and definitions at the end of the monograph aims to help navigate through the narrative and arguments of this study. An introduction to international law generally and international human rights law specifically is included as a separate appendix. It is also recommended that non-legal-specialists read this before reading the body of the monograph.

Part One

THEORIZING PEOPLE POWER IN INTERNATIONAL LAW: GENERAL PRINCIPLES OF HUMAN RIGHTS

Chapter I

People Power and Human Rights: Review and Critique of the Relevant Literature

P art 1 lays out the foundation for the analytical framework developed in this monograph, drawing on three relatively distinct lines of scholarship: 1) efforts to modernize customary law to take account of human rights; 2) preliminary attempts to incorporate non-state actors in the formation of international law, particularly customary law; and 3) efforts to explain the nature of general principles as a source of international human rights law. After giving an overview, the text explores the limitations of each particular line of scholarship and the positive insights that may be gleaned from it for the analytical framework developed here.

First, however, this part begins by examining the central difficulty in developing an international law of human rights—namely, state compliance—and relates this back to the natural law origins of the idea of human rights.

The Problem of a Generally Applicable Positive Law of International Human Rights

The subject area of international human rights has been bedeviled by the problem of state compliance, or lack thereof. The anxiety that international law is not really law and that states comply with it only when it is in their interest to do so is amplified almost to neurosis when it comes to human rights.

To briefly summarize the problem, the international law of human rights is dominated by conventional law in the form of multilateral treaties, but this framework has obvious limitations. Since they are only binding on signatory states, treaties do not bind states that have not signed onto them. Moreover, as with all treaties, states may enter reservations that exempt them from respecting particular treaty provisions, so long as these reservations do not defeat the "object and purpose" of the treaty. Many states have entered important, and quite broad, reservations to human rights treaties, creating a patchwork of coverage. Most treaties have weak enforcement mechanisms, mostly limited to compliance oversight by an independent committee, the decisions of which do not have binding legal authority.

In view of the weaknesses of the conventional international law of human rights, many scholars have by default turned to customary law, the traditional source of generally applicable international law. In addition to filling the gaps left by the patchwork coverage of human rights treaties, a customary law of human rights would facilitate the process of internalizing international law in domestic law, because a significant number of state constitutions incorporate customary international law into domestic legal frameworks and give it a superior status, whereas most constitutions place treaties and statutes on an equal plane.[51]

Notwithstanding the desirability of a customary law of human rights, it has long been recognized that traditional customary law does not translate well to the subject matter area of human rights. Traditional customary law is created through a widespread and consistent pattern of state practice, undertaken with a sense of legal obligation (*opinio juris*) (see Glossary and Appendix). The existence of a norm is derived through an inductive analysis that begins by observing state practice and then generating a rule. Thus, technically, we could only say a customary norm of human rights had emerged when human rights were already being consistently respected by the majority of the states. The problem that a customary rule of human rights was intended to solve—of states not respecting their human rights obligations—would already have to be largely solved in order for a customary rule to form.

Some scholars and jurists have attempted to overcome this conundrum by arguing for a distinction between "modern" (or "instant") and "traditional" customary law, with the former placing less importance on practice and more importance on *opinio juris*. This monograph will discuss these efforts to modernize custom, but first it is useful to reflect on the underlying reason that human rights present such difficulties in terms of sources.

Human Rights, Natural Law, and the Law of Nations

Most scholars, jurists, and activists in the human rights tradition understand human rights to be derived from natural rights, and in turn, they understand that natural rights were initially derived from natural law. In a contrarian account, Moyn disagreed with this more standard view, but his disagreement is predicated on a narrow definition of human rights as the legal doctrine recognized in the framework system of international human rights positive law.[52] Over and over, in various instruments, human rights are declared to be "equal and inalienable." Human dignity is called "inherent," and human beings are said to be "born free and equal in dignity and rights."[52] In his famous dissenting opinion in the *South-West Africa Cases*, Judge Tanaka of the ICJ spelled out the ramifications in terms of law as follows:

> The existence of a human right does not depend on the will of a State; neither internally on its law or on any other legislative measure, nor internationally on treaty or custom, in which the express or tacit will of a State constitutes the essential element. A State or States are not capable of creating human rights by law or by convention; they can only confirm their existence and give them protection. The role of the State is no more than declaratory.[53]

If human rights are rights that inhere in, or in some way flow from, humanness, by definition they cannot derive from positive law.[54] However, this view of human rights is difficult, if not impossible, to ground outside of the theological context of natural law.

Historically, the notion of natural law is associated most closely with the Catholic intellectual tradition, but it has roots that reach back to ancient Rome. In a classic definition, the Roman orator Cicero said that "[t]rue law is right reason in agreement with nature; it is of universal application, unchanging and everlasting.... there will not be different laws at Rome and at Athens, or different laws now and in the future, but one eternal and unchangeable law will be valid for all nations and all times..." This law is superior to every positive law, because "[w]e cannot be freed from its obligations by senate or people." The "author" of this law, "its promulgator, and its enforcing judge" is God. To apprehend it, "we need not look outside ourselves for an expounder or interpreter," we find it in our minds and hearts, through the use of reason."[55]

During the Enlightenment, belief in natural law gave rise to belief in natural rights, and the concept of "rights" crystalized into political and legal reality, culminating in the two great Enlightenment rights proclamations, the US Declaration of Independence and the French Declaration on the Rights of Man and the Citizen.[56] These rights declarations accompanied revolutionary movements for more politically representative governments and limits on sovereign power.

Although the early law of nations applied principles from natural law to the study of international relations, the maturing field of international law gradually distanced itself from natural law and ultimately repudiated it almost completely. As laws of nature came to be interpreted in scientific, rather than theological, terms natural law fell out of favor as a source of international law. Without the grounding of natural law in a theological cosmos, most jurists came to suspect that believers in natural law "were in fact spinning the web of a system out of their own brains as if they were legislators of the world."[57] Gradually, natural law became a subject of interest mainly to moral philosophers and Catholics, not international lawyers generally.

In the area of international law, the positivist turn in the late-19th century resulted in the view that the law could be brought into existence only through state practice, in the form of custom or convention. Thus, the positivist Kelsen saw the natural law allusions in the UDHR as defects, complaining that the declaration in Article 1 that "all human beings are born free and equal" is a "specific natural law doctrine" that is "far from being generally accepted."[58] He found it "not very fortunate" that the opening of the UDHR "thus places the whole document under the sway of a highly disputed doctrine."[59] Human rights could be seen as a residual holdover from the now-abandoned natural law roots of international law, haunting the field like a wandering, unhappy ghost from the past.

"Modernizing" Customary International Law

Turning now to the first line of relevant scholarship, valiant efforts have been made to identify a source in positive law for human rights, notwithstanding their relation to natural law, primarily through efforts to "modernize" customary international law.[60] As noted, traditionally, a customary norm emerges when there is consistent state practice undertaken with a sense of legal obligation. It has been described as being "evolutionary" and "identified through an inductive process" that begins by identifying "specific instances of state practice," together with their underlying justifications, until a pattern is discerned from which it can be said that states are acting in accordance with a perceived rule of law.[61] In contrast, "modern custom" is said to be "derived by a deductive process that begins with general statements of rules rather than particular instances of practice."[62] In a somewhat overlapping argument, Schachter has argued that the evidence used in determining customary international human rights law must be different from the evidence for customary international law in general, and he suggested including statements by state officials condemning human rights violations as breaches of international law; United Nations (UN) resolutions and declarations stating duties arising out of the UDHR; dicta from the ICJ in the Barcelona Traction case,[63] as well as national constitutions and domestic laws implementing human rights treaties and domestic court judgments referring to the UDHR as a source of binding law [64]

The search for an alternative to traditional custom has also led scholars and jurists to argue for the emergence of a new type of non-derogable norm of international law, called *jus cogens*, or "peremptory norms." Small in number, these are said to be norms that are so fundamental that their violation admits no justification, such as the prohibition on the aggressive use of force. *Jus cogens* norms made their first formal appearance in international law in Article 53 of the Vienna Convention on the Law of Treaties (1969), under which it is stated that a treaty is void "if, at the time of its conclusion, it conflicts with a peremptory norm of general international law."[65] *Jus cogens* norms have been criticized for lacking foundation and for their *sui generis* quality: they are like custom in that they are generally applicable, but they are unlike custom in that they are not based on state consent.[66] It has been questioned whether they exist outside of the treaty context.[67]

A variation on *jus cogens* was presented by Henkin in 1994. He argued that, with the emergence of an international human rights regime, an entirely new source of international law had come into being, which he alternatively called "constitutional" or "non-conventional" (in the sense that it does not emerge from conventional law).[68] Taking the legal innovation of *jus cogens* and extending it to all of human rights, not just fundamental rights, he declared that human rights law "is not the result of practice but the product of common consensus from which few dare dissent."[69]

The Trouble with Modern Custom

Efforts to "retrofit" such a foundational component of international law as customary law by changing its criteria and taking away, or diminishing, its most important component (state practice) have made other scholars and jurists distinctly uncomfortable, even if they are in sympathy with the overall aims of the human rights project.[70] In a still current analysis done 25 years ago, Simma and Alston mounted a scathing criticism of such innovations, arguing that they stretch the boundaries of custom beyond recognition and give up the advantages of rules derived by induction, namely, that such rules "are hard and solid; they have been carefully hammered out on the anvil of actual, tangible interaction among states, and they allow reliable predictions as to future state behavior."[71]

Fueling the discomfort with theories of "modern" custom is the worry that international law is swinging too far in the direction of "utopia," in the sense of the continuum set out by Kostkenniemi in his book *From Apology to Utopia: The Structure of International Legal Argument* (2006). It is feared that, in moving to a view of custom that places more emphasis on what states say than on what they do, international jurists and scholars are pronouncing as "law" rules that states widely violate in practice. Weisburd expresses the worry as follows: "It makes [no] sense to label as international law rules that many states will not obey and that very few states are willing to enforce against violators. If one were to accept this view, the world would soon witness repeated violations of rules that scholars insisted were legally binding. Thus, the discipline of international law would in effect be describing itself as ineffectual...."[72]

The Trouble with Traditional Custom

Another concern that gives rise to misgivings about "modernizing" custom is the sense that altering the balance of the required elements will only compound the numerous theoretical problems already nagging traditional customary law itself.[73] While Simma and Alston had faith in the solidity of traditional custom, others contend that it is in crisis. Some scholars find customary international law problematic in theory because it is imprecise and arguably circular.[74] Disagreements exist concerning what state practice should be taken into account as evidence of the formation of customary law. Statements by state officials are particularly controversial.[75] There is also disagreement about how much practice is necessary. How many states have to be involved? How consistent does the practice need to be over time? Then there is the practical problem of collecting and assessing all of this evidence for all the countries in the world.

Problems of settling on what state practice is relevant for determining customary international law are likely part of the reason why scholars have not seriously begun to consider individuals as makers of international law. If defining state practice has controversial aspects, it is considered even more controversial to expand the relevant evidence beyond state practice to include the practice of non-state actors. Fidler observes that while it might follow from a liberal approach to international theory that the practice of private persons (natural or legal) should count toward the development of international law, "[s]uch a notion is even more radical than the idea that the State practice of democracies should count more than that of dictatorships or other types of non-liberal States."[76]

Takeaway

From the point of view of theorizing people power, what is most significant about all these efforts to adapt customary law to the subject matter of human rights s that, except for the *sui generis* doctrine of *jus cogens*, they are all state-centric, in that they see only state behavior as capable of generating international legal norms. None of them provides a space in theory for the input of non-state actors. They are all positivist, in that they see only written or otherwise codified law as relevant for determining international norms. Most importantly, though recognizing a certain difficulty related to sources, these efforts to modernize custom all assume that international human rights law is isomorphic with international law generally, rather than recognizing that it has a different structure, in that it is oriented more toward the state-to-individual relationship than the state-to-state relationship.

Study of this line of scholarship provides certain insights nonetheless. Not all attempts to modernize custom are equally vulnerable to the criticism that they are putting the cart of *opinio juris* before the horse of state practice. The compelling arguments of Schachter and Henkin that domestic constitutions and laws may be a source for international human rights law will be useful in making the case that international human rights law is a hybrid between international and domestic law, with a bidirectional potential for interaction. Provided they are actually enforced, domestic constitutions and laws implementing international human rights, as well as domestic court decisions referencing international human rights law, are not purely verbal or "ineffectual" affirmations but represent hard evidence that international human rights law is being internalized into domestic legal systems.

However, rather than following Henkin, the analytical framework developed in this monograph resists embracing *jus cogens* as currently theorized, out of respect for positivists' concern that it may amount to little more than an airy invention of a creative legal mind. At the same time, *pace* Schachter, it also questions whether customary law, however modernized, is best suited as a framework for taking account of human rights law as resulting from the *jurisgenesis* of people power movements. Traditional custom probably should be abandoned, not modernized, with respect to international human rights law. This is because it is primarily aimed at stabilizing interstate relations through developing predictable rules to organize and predict interactions among states. Hybridity is inherent in the logic of international human rights law, which is not primarily about regulating interstate relations but about regulating intrastate relations between the state and individuals, and which emerged historically from the rights guaranteed in national constitutions.

Drawing on these efforts to modernize customary international law but taking them in a different direction, the monograph takes an approach that attempts to be both principled and pragmatic. Principled, because it affirms a natural law view of human rights as existing prior to, or apart from, positive law. Pragmatic, because it takes the view that natural law needs to be grounded in some kind of practice, even if not the practice of states. If human rights inhere in humanness, human beings and their practices are their proper source.

Theories of Non-State-Centric Customary Law

The next line of scholarship to examine is the effort to theorize individuals as a source of law. In contrast to the wealth of literature generated by the project of "modernizing" custom, scholarship here is sparse. With a few notable exceptions, it is difficult to find scholars or jurists thinking outside of a state-centric perspective on international law. Only a small, dissenting group of scholars has attempted to theorize a more direct role for individuals in international law. Relevant literature is further limited because this monograph's focus on international human rights results in exclusion of efforts to theorize other types of non-state actors, such as corporations or terrorist groups, on the grounds that corporations are not properly the bearers of human rights because they are not human (notwithstanding some judicial and international tribunal decisions to the contrary), and terrorist groups do not acknowledge or respect core human rights principles.

Individuals in civil society have been understood to impact international law in two, mainly indirect ways. First, when organized into civil society organizations (CSOs), they can play a variety of roles with respect to international treaties, including information gathering, advocating, monitoring, and appraising.[77] If states permit, human rights-related CSOs provide their input into the making of international human rights treaties. Typically, this occurs through a consultative process, whereby states confer with CSOs to learn their views on pending legal developments.[78] Rarely, CSOs participate directly in the drafting process, as occurred in the drafting of the International Labor Organization (ILO) conventions.[79] As an international organization, the ILO is unique in that states are required to send representatives from the business and labor communities as delegates, in addition to state representatives, although the state itself decides on who the delegates for business and labor will be. Whether direct or indirect, participation of CSOs in conventional international lawmaking occurs at the discretion of states. Rarely, CSOs can propose international standards that are incorporated into domestic law.[80] The role of nonviolent movements in shaping international law in this indirect way has not been studied or theorized.

Second, individuals can indirectly influence international law by bringing individual complaints in international human rights forums and raising issues of international law in lawsuits in domestic courts. Through these processes, individuals and their representatives can contribute to the development of international law in particular regional and subject matter areas. As this second way of influencing international law does not bear directly on lawmaking, it is not the subject of further discussion here.

New Haven School

Scholars in the so-called New Haven School have broken ground in the direction of a non-state-centric international law. They were ahead of their time in acknowledging the role of individuals in the formation of international law and in identifying human dignity as the normative objective of all international law. They have been criticized, not altogether unfairly, for identifying human dignity with US national interests.[81] As well, their conception of dignity includes the pursuit of wealth and power, making it something of an outlier among theories of dignity in human rights.

Scholars in the New Haven School argued for the recognition of the role of individuals based on the rationale that individuals are already participating in the formation of international law, for example, in review of elite decisions. As expressed by Paust, "From our perspective, the question is not whether individuals participate, but who is participating in the shaping of attitudes and behavior, where, when, how, with what resources, and with what short-term effects and long-term consequences."[82]

Paust has amassed overwhelming evidence of past practice showing that it is "irrefutable" "that traditional international law, even through the early 20th century, recognized roles, rights, and duties of nations, tribes, peoples, belligerents, and other entities and communities in addition to the state."[83] He cautions against the misrecognition that results from a focus on the state:

> [B]y focusing on the "state," one is less likely to appreciate the roles that are actually played by individuals and groups in the formation and continuation of a process involving the denomination "state" and the creation of law both within and outside the state. In a real sense, the state has existed and will exist, as will other forms of human association, because of patterns of human expectation and behavior.[84]

Wilson has elaborated this point in arguing that people power plays a role in state formation, both at the "front end" (when the state is forming) and at the "back end" (when the state or its government is facing large-scale civil resistance).[85] Using the insight from civil resistance studies that people power sustains the state through its life-cycle, she developed the notion of a "dormant social contract" that may be activated during large-scale civil resistance movements as the people systematically withdraw consent from governmental authorities. This withdrawal of consent rebuts the presumption that the state or government has the "acquiescence" of the population that is the predicate for recognition in the international system.

Civil Society

The impact of individuals on international law has been most studied with respect to formal CSOs, though this area of scholarship is still not large. Keck and Sikkink have identified transnational advocacy networks of civil society advocates who were collaborating to influence international relations and law.[86] Glasius has documented the role of CSOs in conceiving the idea of an international criminal court and in influencing negotiations at every stage of the process.[87] From a legal perspective, the most comprehensive analysis has been from Charnovitz, who has documented "two centuries of participation" of nongovernmental organizations (NGOs) in international lawmaking.[88] In this literature, the focus is mainly on indirect effects.

Some scholars have attempted to argue that CSOs should be given a formal role in lawmaking. Gunning proposed a certification process for CSOs similar to that used by the United Nations Economic and Social Council (UNECOSOC) in granting consultative status to CSOs; they argued that CSOs meeting the criteria should be seen as participants "on a par with states" in determining the content of customary international law.[89] Their suggestion has been criticized on the grounds that CSOs are by nature unrepresentative and that the UN consultative status process contains biases that result in marginalization of CSOs from the Global South.[90] The unaccountability of non-state actors is also a concern.[91] Mueller has proposed replacing customary international law (which is limited to the "customs of the community of states") with "customary transnational law," which draws on "the customs of the international community at large," defined as including both global governance and inputs from civil society.[92] Scholarship on transnational law is promising but so far has focused on how transnational law undermines state sovereignty, rather than on the question of how it generates sovereign power alternative to that of states.

Beliefs and Expectations

Ochoa is almost alone in attempting to go beyond the actions of CSOs and to lay the theoretical groundwork for recognizing individuals as makers of international law, particularly international human rights law.[93] Working within the framework of customary law, she finds social and philosophical foundations in globalization;

cosmopolitanism and cosmopolitan citizenship; transnationalism, the subaltern and "globalization from below"; and "participatory democracy"[94] to support what she downplays as the "relatively modest assertion of liberal democratic theory" that "people ought to participate in making the law that governs and protects them."[95] As a kind of counterpart to the requirement of *opinio juris* in traditional state-centric customary law, she argues that the "beliefs and expectations" of individuals should be taken into account in determining customary international law and critically examines four suggestions that have been made as to how to glean "world public opinion"—General Assembly Resolutions, NGOs as proxies for individuals, human rights litigation, and public opinion polls.[96] She leaves aside the question of practice for future debates.

Takeaway

This visionary line of scholars provides several additional insights useful for theorizing people power. Through his excavation of the past, Paust has shown that up until the early-20th century, states recognized individuals and groups in international law in a variety of ways; e.g., they negotiated treaties with subnational groups and assumed that the law of nations rested on the consent of all mankind. Though he does not make the point himself, it is implicit in his analysis that the triumph of positivism is mainly responsible for occluding the role of non-state actors in international law that existed in earlier centuries. With the repudiation of natural law, international law closed off a source of law that was an avenue of input for non-state actors, if only abstractly in the sense of "humanity" in general, or "public conscience." It was after all the natural rights tradition that animated civil resistance movements for popular sovereignty, freedom from slavery, women's suffrage, limitation of working hours and betterment of working conditions. In purging international law of the natural rights tradition, the positivists erased the pathway through which nonviolent movements could potentially have been seen as a source of law.

As for the New Haven School approach, the main problem is that the potential seen for the participation of individuals is not deep or profound. Indeed, acquiescence is the main mode of participation New Haven scholars identify.[97] These scholars find it useful to break down the decision-making process, including at the international level, into seven components: intelligence, promotion or recommendation, prescription, invocation, application, termination, and appraisal.[98] Of these seven, the two that most involve making and enforcing laws are "prescription" and "application." McDougal et al. admit only a "very small, though hopefully representative group"[99] of individuals can directly participate in these functions. For example, in the famous justification of US nuclear testing off the Pacific Islands, McDougal invoked "community expectations" but gave them no more content than a few arguments from international law about the expectations of states, the relevant community appearing to be limited to that anarchical society.

The New Haven School is also vulnerable to the criticism of subjectivism made of natural law for its "speedy descent from the high ground of general principles to the valley of 'self-evident' results"[100] and perhaps most seriously that of policy expediency. In the words of one early critic voicing a harsh interpretation, "Law is policy. Policy is human dignity. Human dignity is fostered in the long run by the success of American foreign policy. Therefore, law is the handmaiden of the national interest of the United States."[101] A policy perspective in favor of human dignity but decentered from the state system would obviate this criticism.

Ochoa lays a more concrete foundation for theorizing people power, in setting forth normative grounds for taking individuals into account. The main limitation of her work is that she confines her analysis to an analogue of the *opinio juris* prong of customary international law and leaves the question of practice for future development by other scholars. But in leaving practice aside, she weakens her argument, since even with respect to traditional state-centric customary law, state practice is considered to be the most essential and determinative prong of customary international law. She also does not address the concern about "ineffectuality" identified above that has been expressed about attempts to modernize custom.

However, building on her work will enable us to demonstrate discursive, theoretical and practical openings for incorporating the practice of individuals and groups into the analysis and practice of international lawmaking. If one were to extend her argument, nonviolent movements that are representative of a broader society and its grievances and aspirations could constitute another important source for domestic and global public opinion. More importantly, nonviolent movements are an objectifiable practice. Ochoa's apparent reason for leaving practice aside is that it may be more difficult and controversial to determine what individual practice "counts." Establishing what counts as a relevant practice will engender debates that "will be important and surely will be prolonged."[102] But Chenoweth and Stephan have shown that it is possible to operationalize civil resistance movements and see them as *sui generis* and distinct from other collective phenomena such as armed or violent movements or movements and campaigns that rely on institutional or traditional means of instituting political change through elections, party politics or courts. Though not without assessment problems of their own, civil resistance movements are more visible, tangible, and objective than "thoughts" and "beliefs," thus easier to count and take account of. They also point toward a greater level of commitment and engagement on the part of individuals, thus giving movements and their activities greater weight as evidence of norm shaping or making.

General Principles

Theoretical difficulties with modern custom as an alternative source for general human rights law have led some scholars, including this author, to turn to general principles, the third source of law identified in Art. 38 of the ICJ Statute.[103] But general principles present no easy solution, as almost everything about general principles as a source of law remains controversial.[104] One recent study concludes that there exists "no consensus on its exact nature and scope, as well as what distinguishes it from other sources of law."[105] Another finds a "doctrinal consensus,"[106] yet states at the same time that the doctrine is "highly controversial and largely neglected."[107] Recently, it has been argued that general principles as a source of law are evolving contextually, so that different methodologies are being used in different areas of law.[108] In jurisprudence, general principles as a source of law are considered methodologically muddy—in its majority opinions, the ICJ inconsistently refers to "principles," "fundamental principles," "generally recognized principles," "basic principles," and "time-hallowed principles," or even "concepts."[109] Perhaps owing to this methodological uncertainty, some scholars demote general principles to "subsidiary means" like judicial decisions, despite their being on an equal plane with treaty and custom according to Article 38.[110]

This methodological muddiness seems deeply built-in. As noted above, the language of Art. 38 ("general principles of law recognized by all civilized nations") was a compromise negotiated during the drafting process between those advocating for a natural law approach and those insisting that general principles derive only from domestic law. Review of the relevant literature reveals at least six distinct approaches:

1) A purely domestic law approach: identifying features that are common to the main legal systems of the world;[111] probably the least controversial use of general principles. This comparative approach to general principles is often, though not always, used to fill technical and procedural gaps in international law with doctrines like estoppel, unjust enrichment, necessity, and proximate cause;[112]

2) A mixed domestic–international positive law approach: this is similar to 1), except that the borrowed features are modified slightly to adapt to the peculiarities of the international legal system;

3) A purely international positive law approach: through an inductive process looking at state practice and the practice of international organizations, identifying features that emerge purely at the international level, like sustainable development;[113] this approach is difficult to distinguish from some "modern" variants of customary international law;[114]

4) A purely natural law approach: declaring certain features as law without reference to positive law, either because such features are intuitively grasped, or reflect a "common conscience";[115]

5) A mixed natural law–domestic positive law approach: reflecting the view that "principles common to legal systems often reflect natural law principles that underlie international law";[116]

6) A logical or inherent legal approach: identifying features logically necessary to, or inherent in, any legal system, legal instrument, or law itself; this includes an approach focused specifically on identifying features inherent or logically necessary to the functioning of international law, such as the principle of diplomatic protection.[117]

With respect to human rights law specifically, there exists in the scholarly literature a perception that "general principles of human rights" exist, but little systemic exposition exists of what these "general principles of human rights" might be. They are often merely invoked as if they were self-evident.[118] To the extent they are given content, it is often through reference to the UDHR.[119] Because the UDHR is the "mother" instrument of international human rights law, this makes a certain amount of sense. However, except for the principle of nondiscrimination, the UDHR does not articulate principles; it merely enumerates a basic set of rights, at least 30, and arguably many more. In the specific context of criminal justice, Bassiouni describes a methodology of comparing the congruence of rights found in national constitutions with rights found in international human rights instruments in order to determine general principles of human rights: "The rights found in the instruments evidence their international recognition, while their counterparts in the national constitutions evidence national legal recognition. The congruence of both indicate the existence of a 'general principle.' "[120] This corresponds to the second approach described above.

Simma and Alston made a case for general principles as a source of international human rights law in the same article where they rejected "modern" custom. After arguing persuasively for the human rights practice of the UN bodies and specialized agencies as an authoritative interpretation of the human rights provisions of the UN Charter, they questioned whether it can be presumed that all of the rights enumerated in the UDHR, as well as new rights like the right to development, can be "said to fall within the ambit of the original Charter provision." They then turned to general principles as an ultimate solution to the problem of a generally applicable human rights law, reinterpreting UN practice as evidence of "general principles," rather than customary law. According to their view, general principles do not need to detour through domestic legal systems; they only need to have objective recognition, which can emerge directly in international law.

Simma and Alston's solution has not been widely accepted because, in practice, reliance on UN practice turns out to be almost indistinguishable from the new forms of custom that they rejected. As they themselves note, "Of course, if we perceive customary international law to be derived not only from a generalization of State practice but from the express articulation of rules in, for example, declarations of the General Assembly, the concept of [modern] custom will be difficult to distinguish from that of general principles recognized internationally in the first instance."[121] Still, they argue for the benefit of keeping customary law and general principles distinct, "on the ground… that the concept of a 'recognized' general principle seems to conform more closely than the concept of custom to the situation where a norm invested with strong inherent authority is widely accepted even though widely violated."[122] This monograph agrees with Simma and Alston's suggestion that general principles is the most theoretically coherent source of human rights law. However, their theorization of general principles falls short, because it collapses into "modern custom."

Takeaway

Using general principles as a matrix for incorporating individuals into international law is preferable to customary law because it side steps the methodological debates about the elements of customary law. It could be reasonably objected that customary law has so many unsettled elements that it should not be expanded further and that the inductive process for deriving customary law is already so difficult and so controversial that it would face insuperable theoretical challenges to expand it in order to include people power movements. Working within the logic of general principles as a source of law means that development of a *demos*-centric international human rights law can proceed without impacting the debates regarding customary international law.[123]

Adopting the general principles matrix entails that we use general principles in a general and a specific sense. The general sense refers to how general principles are used in Article 38 of the ICJ Statute (as category or type of source for law), while general principles in a specific sense defines the content of the category in a particular subject matter area of law—in this case, human rights law. In the specific sense, this monograph identifies four such general principles—nondiscrimination, nonrepression, nonexploitation, and nonviolence—relevant to the human rights law and analyzes them in greater detail below.

General principles as a source of law remain unsettled doctrinally; this leaves scope for innovation. As they are not defined purely in terms of state action, nothing precludes them from incorporating the actions of non-state actors as makers of law. While general principles are often used to fill in gaps in international law, nothing limits them to procedural doctrines. They are also useful because, at least in principle, they have a hybrid structure, potentially cross-cutting international and domestic law, as well as natural law and positive law. As Biddulph and Newman note, general principles "are inherently flexible, able to transpose legal ideas from one system to another...."[124]

But though general principles potentially encompass natural law, there is little in the scholarly literature developing this point, because natural law in general has fallen away as a living tradition for international lawyers. As noted at the beginning of this part, what also sets human rights apart from other subject matter areas in international law is that they are a natural law idea, not deriving their authority from the positive law. But while natural law is recognizable to international lawyers in a historical sense, there is at present no body of natural law that is used independently of the positive law to adjudicate claims related to human rights violations, except perhaps for the controversial notion of *jus cogens*.

This monograph puts forward the original proposition that civil resistance movements function as a proxy for the content of natural law and explains how in more detail in Part II. In the pre-positivist history of international law, natural law was a way for jurisprudents to acknowledge "mankind," "humanity," and "the dictates of conscience" in pronouncing international law. In other words, in referring to natural law, early international scholars were invoking the "beliefs" and "opinions" of individuals that Ochoa is trying to recognize. Individuals and movements striving to realize human rights often operate outside of, or prior to, established legal or institutional frameworks, using the extra-legal means of civil disobedience, noncooperation, stay-aways, and demonstrations. Such individuals are engaged in *jurisgenesis*, the cultural process of imagining and creating a normatively alternative sociopolitical and legal order reflecting their ideals of justice, including equality, dignity, and freedom. A main thrust of this monograph therefore is to develop a workable framework that will ultimately facilitate the operationalizing of the natural law reflected in civil resistance movements. This can then be objectified, conceptually extrapolated and eventually made usable for an inclusive and multicultural international legal system that would accommodate people not only as an agency of law shaping but lawmaking.

While complicated, devising an inductive process for determining the input of people power movements to general principles of human rights does not present insuperable methodological problems. However, it will require close collaboration between legal scholars and social scientists studying civil resistance and movements. Empirical research is of course already being done on human rights in general, particularly focusing on the impact of treaty ratification on the human rights behavior of states. Arguably, civil resistance movements lend themselves more readily to empirical research than human rights violations, because such movements have many "visible" markers, whereas many human rights violations are carried out in secret. Large protests, or strikes, or even consistently recurring smaller protests, street theatre, "flash mobs," are observable, especially in today's world of cell phone and social media access, whereas torture for example usually occurs in secret and is shrouded in official denials. Empty buses during the US civil rights struggle illustrated a powerful tactic in action—boycott of segregated public transportation—though of course some nonviolent tactics, like work or production slow-down, may be relatively less visible.

Quantitative study has shown that people power can be operationalized. In their study *Why Civil Resistance Works*, Chenoweth and Stephan created the Nonviolent and Violent Campaigns and Outcomes (NAVCO) dataset.[125] Using specific criteria to identify civil resistance campaigns (see this monograph's Glossary of Terms), they focused on campaigns having "maximalist" aims, meaning that the campaign aimed to change a governmental regime, expel a foreign military occupation force, or create a new state through secession. In creating the first version of the dataset (NAVCO 1.0) covering the timeframe from 1900 to 2006, they began with an extensive review of the literature on nonviolent civil resistance and put together an initial list, which they corroborated against encyclopedias, case studies, and a comprehensive bibliography compiled by experts on nonviolent civil resistance. For the violent campaigns, they referred to existing databases on violent conflicts. They cross-checked their conclusions with experts in the field. Finally, they refined their list to include only "maximalist" campaigns.

Chenoweth has been continually updating and refining the NAVCO database, which has been used with a growing frequency by social scientists. The third version (NAVCO 3.0) has been utilized in a study expanding understanding of the factors that lead movements to succeed or fail in the crucial activity of maintaining nonviolent discipline.[126] Chenoweth is now working on a new dataset that will include "reformist" campaigns, like those discussed in Part IV of the monograph, which stay within the existing legal framework of the state and seek its reform.

Methodologically, a general principles approach to international human rights would have some similarities to regular customary international law, except that it would give significant weight to the activities of people power movements reflecting a human rights *ethos*. Inclusion of people power as a source of general principles of international human rights law does not dispense with the effort to create a consensus among states around binding human rights norms, but it supplements that effort with recognition that human rights norms have emerged—and are continuing to develop and evolve—through a bottom-up process whereby ordinary people, often using organized extra-legal means of nonviolent action, are advancing specific norms into political and legal domestic and international realms and creating a new consensus around them. Through more detailed study of how rights function in civil resistance movements, we can begin to codify an international law of human rights based on the relevant practice of states, international and supranational organizations, plus the beliefs and expectations of individuals as well as the people-powered practice through which the agency of individuals is organized toward the realization of the rights they are asserting and claiming.

Chapter II
Analytical Framework

P art II of this monograph takes the insights developed in Part I and uses them to develop an analytical framework to begin creating a *demos-centric* international human rights law and thus lay down the foundations for a theory of nonviolent civil resistance in international law. In developing this analytical framework, it will be useful to separate out two distinct premises: first, international human rights law is a hybrid of international and domestic law; and second, it is a hybrid of positive law and natural law, where natural law is redefined as the *jurisgenesis* of civil resistance movements consistent with the general principles or *ethos* of human rights. As process, natural law encompasses people power. As substance, natural law encompasses rights asserted by people power movements beyond those protected by positive law.

First Premise: Human Rights Law is a Hybrid of International and Domestic Positive Law

In a 1994 Sibley lecture, Henkin said that while international human rights law is an innovation in terms of international law, it draws its substance from the "once-excluded sources" of national domestic laws[127] and thus "derive[s] from national constitutional rights."[128]

This is true, historically and practically. The drafters of the UDHR studied existing national constitutions and other municipal laws from around the world as the starting point for the creation of an international law of human rights. Their usual mode of working was to look to rights guarantees in national constitutions, find patterns and consensus, and draft language for the international declaration that either reflected the best existing language or improved on it.

Furthermore, the relationship to national constitutions was imagined to be bidirectional, and it did in fact become bidirectional, to a significant extent. Despite not including the requirement that it should be implemented in a member state's constitution, "[t]he Universal

Declaration has served as a model or inspiration for numerous constitutional and legislative provisions."[129] Jayawickrama finds that "no fewer than 90 national constitutions drawn up since 1948 contain statements of fundamental rights which, where they do not faithfully reproduce the provisions of the Universal Declaration, are at least inspired by it."[130]

The constitutionalization of international human rights law transposes international law into domestic law, where it becomes susceptible to pressure from individuals, including movements—pressure that is legally meaningful since in a majority of the world's constitutions the people are the holders of sovereignty. As has long been recognized by practicing human rights lawyers, the most effective means for enforcing international human rights law is to ensure that it is "incorporated into the domestic legal system through executive action, judicial interpretation, legislative action, or some combination of the three."[131] Through internalization, international human rights law becomes binding domestic law that state officials are obliged to "obey as part of the domestic legal fabric."[132]

Although legal scholars today usually focus on a process of internalization that moves from international law to domestic law, the drafting history of the UDHR indicates that the process of interaction actually began at the domestic level.

Furthermore, this bidirectionality continues today. Although the basic human rights instruments guarantee freedom of information as part of freedom of expression, no human rights treaty was originally interpreted to mean that states were obligated to enact freedom of information acts (FOIAs) or their equivalents (also known as right to information acts [RTIAs]). However, from 1993 to 2005, the number of states having FOIAs in their domestic legislation more than doubled, from 30 to over 60. From 2005 to 2009, another 30 states enacted such legislation bringing the global total to 90. By 2012, the total was more than 112.[133] The international human right to expression is now understood to require states to adopt FOIAs, or their equivalent.[134]

The relationship between domestic and international law can be visualized as organized around the horizontal axis of a grid (see Box 1), with the top two quadrants representing international law and the bottom two quadrants domestic law. The double-sided arrows bisecting the axis indicate the permeability between international and domestic law—international law is internalized into domestic law, while domestic law shapes the content of international law.

Box 1. The relationship between domestic and international law

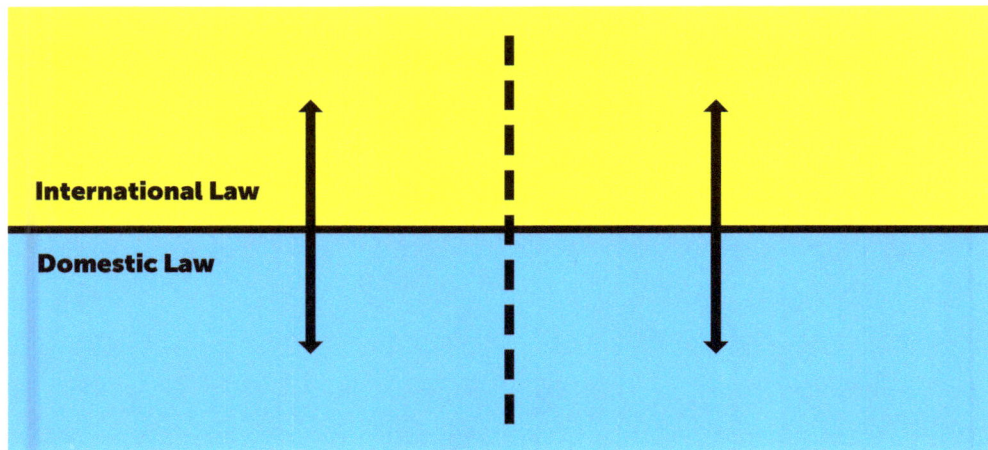

Second Premise: Human Rights Law is a Hybrid of Natural and Positive Law

The second way that international human rights law is hybrid in nature is that it results from both positive and natural law. The historical evidence as to how the UDHR was drafted provides an opening for the effects of non-state actors to be registered in international law. To the extent that the rights provisions in national constitutions resulted, directly or indirectly, from civil resistance movements engaged in human rights *jurisgenesis*, those movements can be considered as having provided indirectly the raw material for the content of the UDHR provisions. Movements whose actions led to the inclusion of the specific rights-based provisions into domestic constitutions, which UDHR drafters adopted, can be said to have impacted international human rights law.

Article 2 of the UDHR, for example, prohibits discrimination on the basis of sex. *Prima facie*, then, women's movements that struggled against this type of discrimination in numerous countries and left visible imprints on their domestic constitutions are also relevant for the emergence of international human rights norms in this field.[135] The actions of US suffragettes were, for example, lawless at times; they demonstrated; they refused to pay taxes; and they picketed the White House. When they were imprisoned for picketing the White House, they were tortured in a "Night of Terror"; they engaged in hunger strikes; and they were force-fed. Susan B. Anthony was criminally charged for voting in the 1872 presidential election when women had not yet won the right to vote. In the speaking tour she undertook in her defense, she rejected the idea that government had the power to give or take away her rights: "The Declaration of Independence, the United States Constitution, the constitutions of the several states and the organic laws of the territories," she argued, "all alike propose to protect the people in the exercise of their God-given rights."[136]

Like the earlier movements that gave rise to the UDHR, today's civil resistance movements are engaged in *jurisgenesis*—collectively imagining an alternative to the current positive legal order and working to bring it into being. Such movements embed specific moral ideas that in turn have incipient legal content. This *jurisgenesis* of civil resistance can be viewed as a natural law that enacts and embeds moral ideas of right and wrong, of justice and fairness, of rights and no-rights, that are either not yet reflected in current laws "on the books" or not yet being enforced and realized. For example, during the phase of the demonstrations in Maidan Square in December 2013 when Ukrainians protested against a decision by their government not to sign a Euro-integration agreement, a protester read a poem, in which he said, "Let evil tyrants tell their tales/And say that we are breaking laws/They'll never make us mute or scared/The sacred truth is our law."[137] By this appeal to a law that is "a sacred truth," Ukrainian protesters, it can be argued, used a natural law frame to legitimize their actions against the president whose own positive law-based legitimacy came from democratic elections held three years earlier but who, in majority of people's views, had betrayed their trust, reneged on their social contract and thus lost formal legitimacy to govern.[138]

In terms of the grid we began constructing earlier, the relationship between natural and positive law can be visualized (see Box 2) as organized around the vertical axis of the grid, with the left two quadrants representing natural law and the right two quadrants positive law. The horizontal arrows bisecting the vertical lines indicate that the *jurisgenesis* can go both ways—people power movements can give rise to positive law, while positive law can engender people power movements.

Box 2. The relationship between natural and positive law

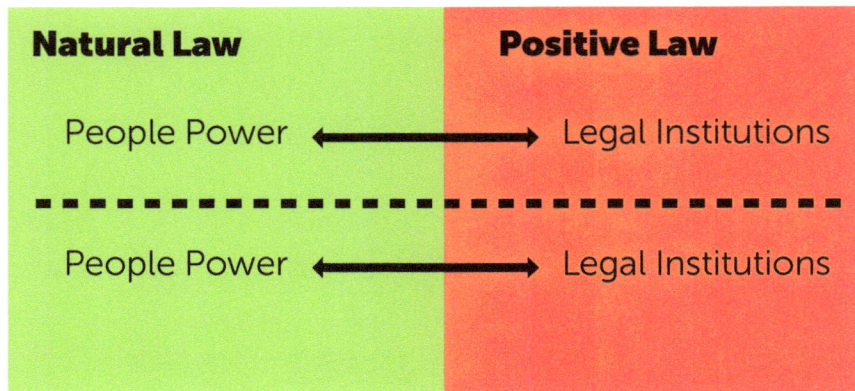

Natural Law	Positive Law
People Power ⟷	Legal Institutions
People Power ⟷	Legal Institutions

To go back to the example of freedom of information laws originating in domestic law, we will not have the complete picture if we focus only on enacted legislation. Non-state actors took a lead role in the rapid spread of FOIAs (or RTIAs) throughout domestic legal systems in recent years. The case of India is notable in the role played by nonviolent civil resistance. The genesis of India's RTIA was a village sit-in in the northwest state of Rajasthan.[139] Local workers had unresolved questions regarding minimum wages, misappropriated benefits, and corruption.[140] From this event, the *Mazdoor Kisan Shakti Sangathan* (MKSS), or Organization for the Power of Laborers and Farmers, was formed, with its principal goal of "demanding information as a right."[141] The MKSS utilized a method conducting village-based public hearings, or *Jan Sunwais*.[142] These hearings gave the power of assigning accountability to the people, rather than relying on a court. Still, the informal hearings had a legitimate structure:

> Every *Jan Sunwai* has a panel of judges with independent credentials, who can ensure that the proceedings are fair, allowing everyone a hearing. The people are a large jury, before whom hiding the truth is, for obvious reasons, more difficult than before the judge in court... Most important of all, this forum breaks the heavy dependence on the Government for redressal. The face to face dialogue brings home very powerfully the need for accountability, and the urgency and importance of citizens participation in matters of governance.[143]

After MKSS gained momentum, its members joined the India Press Council in

1996 and founded the National Campaign for People's Right to Information (NCPRI).[144] That year, the NCPRI sent the government a model FOIA. When the government stalled and ultimately passed a weak law, the opposition Congress Party used the law as a campaign issue and won the election.[145] However, the new government tried to pass the same weak legislation once more. This was met with strong criticism by the media and outcry from members of the public and government. As a result, the new government passed the Right to Information Act in October 2005, one of the most effective in the world.[146]

A similar movement for the right to information played out in neighboring Bangladesh. In other countries, like Indonesia, Guatemala, Yemen, and Jordan, CSOs led the campaign to pass a FOIA, while in still other countries, governments were the main drivers behind enactment of FOIAs in domestic law. The Associated Press recently did a global study of the effectiveness of FOIAs, and the lead researcher and reporter Mendoza recognized the importance of people power even after FOIAs were enacted by summing up the result of the study: "When the citizens rise up and say, we want to have accountability in our government, we want to have transparency, those laws really work. In countries where the law is adopted as a financial incentive, those are the countries we found more often are ignoring them."[147]

Reference to natural law is additionally necessary in theorizing people power because the positive law of human rights described in Part I of this monograph does not encompass all of the rights that could be, and have been, claimed by civil resistance movements, and thus, it is insufficient as a theoretical framework. Consider the landmark General Assembly Resolution, The Declaration on the Right and Responsibility of Individuals, Groups, and Organs of Society to Promote Universally Recognized Human Rights and Fundamental Freedoms (The Declaration on Human Rights Defenders, or DHRD), which provides the following:

> Human rights defenders address any human rights concerns, which can be as varied as, for example, summary executions, torture, arbitrary arrest and detention, female genital mutilation, discrimination, employment issues, forced evictions, access to health care, and toxic waste and its impact on the environment. Defenders are active in support of human rights as diverse as the rights to life, to food and water, to the highest attainable standard of health, to adequate housing, to a name and a nationality, to education, to freedom of movement and

to non-discrimination. They sometimes address the rights of categories of persons, for example women's rights, children's rights, the rights of indigenous persons, the rights of refugees and internally displaced persons, and the rights of national, linguistic or sexual minorities.

Though the list of exemplary human rights mentioned here is not exhaustive, it is striking that there is no mention of self-determination, or national or political liberation, no mention of democracy or of a right to an accountable government; yet these are often precisely the objectives pursued by civil resistance movements. The following are some of the natural rights that are not reflected in state-centric human rights treaties but that are often claimed by movements.

- Right to resist tyranny or oppression
- Right to self-determination (outside of the narrowly defined practice of internal autonomy)
- Right to democracy
- Right to an accountable government

This non-exhaustive list of rights derives from the French and US Declarations and the philosophical writings giving rise to, or justifying, them, such as works by John Locke, the French philosopher, and German philosopher Emmanuel Kant, and from the people's movements they inspired in the 19th-century. However, their origins are for present purposes less important than the fact that they are rights being claimed by nonviolent movements around the world today, even though they are not rights protected by positive law in human rights instruments.

General Principles of Human Rights

One more step is required in creating a framework for theorizing people power: defining the specific content of the general principles that apply to human rights law and function as limiting criteria for human rights *jurisgenesis*. Positive law can be just or unjust. Movements can be radically democratic or hierarchically fascist. In order to create criteria by which positive law and particularly natural law can be understood as furthering the human rights project, we need to define the content of the general princip.es that organize the collective praxis of that project. It will be useful to keep in mind Fitzmaurice's definition of a principle as "something which is not itself a rule, but which underlies a rule, and explains or provides the reason for it."[148] To describe it most parsimoniously, four general principles lie at the heart of the human rights project, namely, nondiscrimination, nonrepression, nonexploitation, and nonviolence. Most of the important human rights protected in positive law and aspired to as natural law by civil resistance movements can arguably be understood as emanating from these core principles.[149]

These four general principles are useful in creating criteria to determine which nonviolent movements to include in the human rights project and which to exclude. Rather than representing a fixed state—particular substantive rights—they are more like vectors that define a direction along which jurisgenerative activity can be organized.

These principles embrace both rights and duties. The duty of nondiscrimination implies the right to be free from discrimination; the duty of nonrepression implies the right to be free from repression, and so on. They combine to create a certain basic narrative or *ethos* that is central to the human rights project, in which human dignity is realized through the means of individual and collective activity organized around the principles of nondiscrimination, nonrepression, nonexploitation, and nonviolence, and that organized activity in turn brings about greater freedom, justice, and peace.[150]

The nature of human rights as rights that flow from humanness does not have to be accepted as an article of religious faith. Rather, it can be seen as part of a socially created hypothesis that treating human beings as if they are sacred beings, with certain inviolable rights, will bring about earthly societies less plagued by violence and suffering. If the natural law of human rights can be reformulated as people power, it will create a way to objectify natural law as a sociological phenomenon.

The Ethos of Human Rights

The human rights *ethos* is textually grounded in the basic human rights instruments. By their terms, the core human rights instruments reflect the ends of "freedom, justice, and peace" and set out respect for human dignity as the means, for example, in the "whereas" clauses in the Preamble to the UDHR:

Whereas recognition of the inherent dignity and of the equal and inalienable rights

of all members of the human family is the foundation of freedom, justice and peace in the world,
Whereas disregard and contempt for human rights have resulted in barbarous acts which have outraged the conscience of mankind...

The preambles to the International Covenant on Civil and Political Rights (ICCPR) and International Covenant on Social, Economic, and Cultural Rights (ICESCR) express the same basic idea in slightly different words:

Considering that, in accordance with the principles proclaimed in the Charter of the United Nations, recognition of the inherent dignity and of the equal and inalienable rights of all members of the human family is the foundation of freedom, justice and peace in the world...

It has been said that, in international human rights law, dignity "provide[s] a unifying creed unto which most nations can agree, even though the exact contours of that creed might not be specifically described."[151] Dignity itself is a kind of secular-religious object of faith at the heart of the human rights idea, denoting the spark of divinity in the human, the priceless worth of every human life. Another way to express the concept of human dignity is the quality of being a "human being" (not an animal or a thing) or the quality of belonging to "humanity." References to dignity or its equivalents pervade the major international human rights instruments. They are found in the UN Charter;[152] in the UDHR;[153] in the ICCPR and ICESCR, and in the Convention on the Elimination of All Forms of Discrimination Against Women (CEDAW), among other treaties and soft law.

Given the centrality of dignity in the human rights legal regime, philosophers are expending efforts to unpack its meaning. Its provenance is generally traced to Kant, who provides language from which perhaps the simplest definition of dignity can be taken. To have dignity means to be treated as an end in oneself, and not as a means to some other end. It is a demand for respect, "and its corollary, the right to defy being treated with disrespect—of which a state's denial of rights and justice is the ultimate manifestation."[154]

In fact, dignity is a term deeply resonant with nonviolent civil resisters around the world. The demand for respect "symbolizes an empowered individual who rejects living a lie (i.e., the fiction that living under censorship, repression, fear is normal), construed from the behavior of an oppressive regime that strips away a person's humanity while insulting his intellect."[155] In Poland, the Solidarity movement held a Congress in 1981, in which it pronounced that "the ultimate goal of Solidarity is to create dignified conditions of life in an economically and politically sovereign Poland. By this we mean a life free from poverty, exploitation, fear and lies, in a democratically and legally organized society."[156] In Arabic, the Tunisian revolution bore the name of "the revolution of freedom and dignity."[157] Crowds in both Tunisia and Egypt shouted "كرامةكرامة كرامة—*Karamah*, *Karamah*, dignity, dignity!"[158] One protester in the Egyptian revolution said, "This isn't 'the January 25th revolution'"—referring to the date when the revolution began—"This is a revolution for dignity."[159] The Euromaidan revolution is called by Ukrainians and known in Ukraine as the "Revolution of Dignity." The nonviolent phase of the Syrian revolution had the grassroots name of the "Dignity Revolution." The September 2015 anticorruption protests that broke out in Moldova were coordinated by a civic movement calling itself "Dignity and Truth." A protester calling for a change of government and end to corruption in Morocco said, "this [was] the people speaking to get its dignity back."[160] A young mother who participated in Lebanon's "You Stink" protests (named after the failure of the government to provide necessary monies for trash pick-up) named her demands as "[e]lectricity, water and dignity... And get these sectarian thieves out. We look at each other as enemies while they are filling their pockets. It's not enough to sit home and complain."[161] "We are tired of the theft from our education, our health care, and the theft of our dignity," said a demonstrator named Vivian, who came to the protest governmental corruption in Guatemala with her two children. "We don't want any more corruption, we want Guatemala to flourish."[162] When a representative from Abahlali baseMjondolo, a grassroots movement of shack dwellers in South Africa, addressed the South African Human Rights Commission, he complained that even when the government talked to the group, "they refuse to talk about dignity or land" and tried instead to "channel the discussion in other directions." Another member of the group complained when a local political official used to come with pots of food to the side of the road: "We said no, we are not dogs, we are not animals, that you have to dish food to and then forget about them, until you remember, oh, we have to go and give food to the shack dwellers again... No, we are not pets, we are human beings. We have to be treated like human beings."[163]

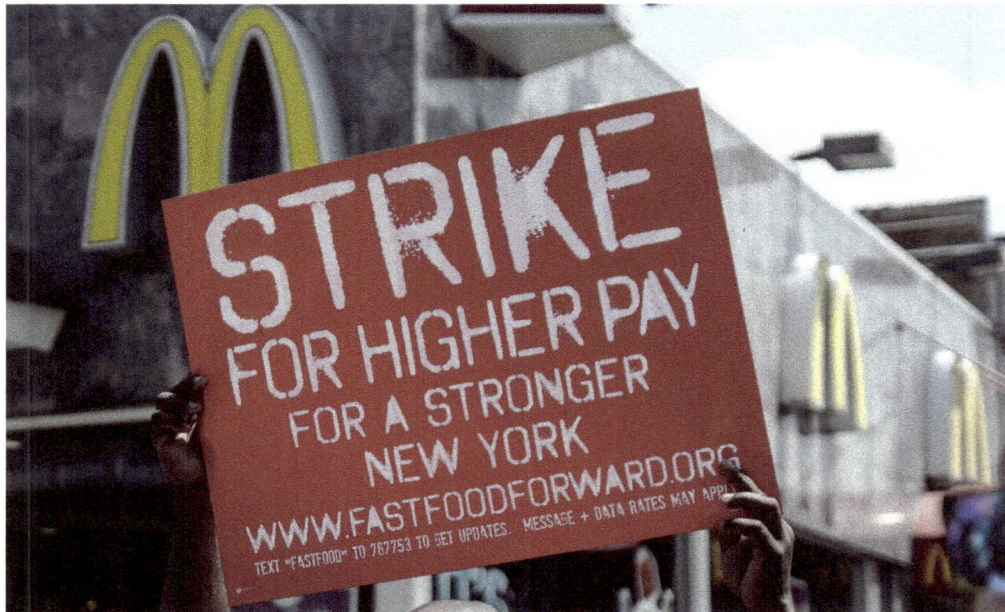

Fast food strike in New York City, July 2013. Source: Flickr user Annette Bernhardt, via Creative Commons.

The Catholic Priest Jozef Tischner, an important intellectual leader of the Polish Independent Self-Governing Trade Union, Solidarity, made the connection between "dignity" and "human rights" explicit in 1980:

> The concept of human dignity defies simple definition. Human dignity is a value that can be seen and felt, the one about which it is difficult to speak. One can, however, turn attention toward this value by pointing out its context. The context of the concept of human dignity is human rights. Human dignity expresses itself through the rights afforded to human beings.[164]

Drawing on Tischner's remarks, human rights *jurisgenesis* can be described as the realization of human dignity through the means of asserting rights and fulfilling duties in accordance with the general principles of nondiscrimination, nonrepression, nonexploitation, and nonviolence. If civil resistance movements manifest these principles, or some of them without negating the others, then arguably it is appropriate to characterize them as human rights movements. These four principles may be further elaborated.

Nondiscrimination

"Nondiscrimination," phrased negatively as a duty, goes centrally to the idea of equality and expresses an imperative to undo invidious social hierarchies and refute justifications for them. Phrased positively as a right, it corresponds to a right to "equal treatment," without regard to contingent, state-dependent facts like nationality or citizenship. "Nondiscrimination" also captures discrimination that affects the enjoyment of other rights, including social and economic rights—for example, when health care is unequally distributed between the rich and the poor. Both the right and the duty of nondiscrimination propel outputs along vectors leading to "justice."

Nondiscrimination is threaded, almost redundantly, through the Articles of the ICCPR and is a general principle reflecting a commitment to equality and universality. The ICCPR prohibits discrimination based on "race, color, sex, language, religion, political or other opinion, national or social origin, property, birth or other status" (Art 2 (1)). The ICCPR separately guarantees the equal rights of men and women to enjoy the rights enumerated in the ICCPR (Art. 3), as well as equality before the courts and tribunals (Art. 14); the equal right to recognition before the law (Art. 16); and the right to equality before the law and to equal protection of the laws (Art. 26). The ICCPR prohibits "advocacy of national, racial or religious hatred" constituting incitement to "discrimination, hostility or violence" (Art. 20). It guarantees the right of political participation without discrimination on the prohibited grounds listed in Article 2 (Art. 25). It provides that children have a right to protection without discrimination on any of the prohibited grounds (Art. 24). Also guaranteed are the rights of "ethnic, religious or linguistic minorities" to enjoy their "own culture, to profess and practice the religion, or to use their own language" (Art. 27).

Examples of how the principle of nondiscrimination might be expressed in nonviolent movements include demands for equality or equal protection of the law (anti-Apartheid), equal access to political rights (women's suffrage), advocacy for groups particularly discriminated against to be treated as equals (Black Lives Matter).

Nonrepression

"Nonrepression" phrased negatively refers to the duties of states and individuals not to repress the political and autonomy rights of others. Phrased positively as rights, nonrepression entails liberty rights, primarily against the state, including rights to privacy and security of one's person, family, home, and correspondence (Art. 17); and freedom of thought, religion and expression (Art. 18). It also encompasses physical integrity rights (the rights to freedom from torture and cruel, inhuman and degrading treatment (Art. 7) and physical liberty rights, like freedom from slavery and forced labor (Art. 8); freedom from debtor's prison (Art. 10); and freedom of movement (Art. 12). The principle of nonrepression requires that due process like the right to a fair trial be fulfilled. It also includes the rights to political participation (Art. 25), as well as the natural rights of resistance to oppression, for democracy, self-determination, and accountable government.

In civil resistance movements, the right to be free from repression could express itself, e.g., through protests against state security apparatuses and policing; against surveillance and monitoring; or through building alternative media and bottom-up means of communication to circumvent censorship and off- and online control. It can also be expressed through demands for democracy or for perpetrators of human rights violations to be held accountable for their acts.

Nonexploitation

Dignity cannot be achieved unless a person has access to "all that is needed for a dignified life."[165] The third principle—nonexploitation—derives from Marx's critique of the natural rights tradition as reinforcing the egoistic man at the center of capitalism. Marx analyzed capitalism as having an inherent tendency to produce instabilities in the form of booms and busts and to result in the progressive immiserization of workers. Though his solution to these problems—the revolution of the proletariat—has been discredited, his critique still has intellectual force. At the time of the drafting of the UDHR, the central question was whether the Western liberal tradition and the Marxist tradition could find common ground. The Marxist political program has been left behind but the values advanced by the tradition—social and economic welfare, the communal good—have been integrated into the human rights movement with the adoption of the ICESCR, especially after an Optional Protocol came into force in 2013. Without the principle of nonexploitation, the human rights project maps too neatly onto political liberalism and corporate capitalism, exposing the project to the criticism of neoimperialism or neocolonialism. However, the most radical vision of the human rights project, the UDHR, conceived of human rights as an indivisible and interdependent unity of civil and political rights and social and economic rights.

The general principle of nonexploitation encompasses most of the social and economic rights outlined in the ICESCR, including the right to work (Art. 6); the right to "just and favorable conditions of work" (Art. 7), including fair wages, safe and healthy working conditions, rest and leisure; the right to form and join trade unions (Art. 8); the right to social security and social insurance (Art. 9); special protections for childbirth (Art. 10); "the right of everyone to an adequate standard of living for himself and his family, including adequate food, clothing and housing, and to the continuous improvement of living conditions" (Art. 11); the right to the "enjoyment of the highest attainable standard of physical and mental health" (Art. 12); the right to education (Art. 13); the right to share in cultural life and scientific progress, including to benefit from any intellectual property (Art. 15). Nonexploitation includes structural exploitation (e.g., an unfair tax code) and exploitation by businesses or other private actors. Social and economic rights are here expressed through the idea of not exploiting in order to highlight human responsibility for human suffering.

Although it has been said that "tough questions" remain about the ability of nonviolent campaigns to bring about changes to the structural foundations of the economy,[166] the same is true, perhaps even more true, of the human rights project in general. In the end, it may be that social, economic, and cultural rights may be most effectively realized through nonviolent civil resistance, rather than through formal human rights mechanisms. There is a precedent in the past. For example, at the end of the 19th-century, when the government first began to track working hours, the average employee in the manufacturing industries worked 100 hours per week. The standard 8-hour work day of today was achieved through civil resistance campaigns led by workers and their families.[167]

Nonviolence

While the principles of nondiscrimination, nonrepression, and nonexploitation are drawn from the human rights instruments, especially the International Bill of Rights,[168] the fourth and final principle—nonviolence—has thus far not been theorized by human rights scholars and activists. Nevertheless, nonviolence—understood as acting without threat or use of violence—has an important and even special place in human rights practice. Article 5 of the Declaration on Human Rights Defenders provides that, for the purpose of promoting and protecting such rights and freedoms, "everyone has the right, individually and in association with others, at the national and international levels: (a) To meet or assemble *peacefully* (italics added)."[169] The definition used by the special rapporteur on human rights defenders makes the use of nonviolent means part of the "minimum standards" necessary for determining who is a human rights defender. In other words, one cannot use violent means and be considered a human rights defender.[170] Amnesty International, justly credited with a pivotal role in bringing human rights to the attention of the world, defines its powerfully symbolic category of "prisoners of conscience" as "people who have been jailed because of their political, religious or other conscientiously-held beliefs, ethnic origin, sex, color, language, national or social origin, economic status, birth, sexual orientation or other status, *provided that they have neither used nor advocated violence*" (italics added).

Nonviolence is also a core principle because the use of force in the name of human rights does not respect the right to life.[171] Not all nonviolent resistance practice is a human rights practice but there is compelling argument that all human rights practice must be nonviolent. It is important that the means used to realize rights be consistent with the overall spirit and end goals of the human rights project. Although not all violence is categorically rejected in international law—the UN Charter justifies armed defense in case of armed aggression while the "just war" doctrine sees attaining peace as a proper end goal of war. However, from a human rights perspective, resistance characterized by a high degree of nonviolent discipline is the appropriate modality for realizing human rights because it is less likely to set off a costly cycle of violence in the short and long term and less likely than its violent counterpart to increase the level of repression, discrimination and exploitation. According to scholarly findings, "nonviolent campaigns were far more—almost 10 times more—likely to usher in more peaceful and democratic order than violent insurgencies."[172] A 2005 report from Freedom House found that the nonviolent nature of transition was the "key factor in building durable democracies."[173] At the same time, external armed interventions tend to extend the duration of civil wars[174] and even worse, increase the number of civilians killed.[175] A country has a more than 40 percent chance of relapsing into civil war within 10 years if the conflict is resolved through violent means.[176] Even a military strategist, such as Col. Helvey who sees nonviolent conflict as "a form of warfare," advances arguments in support of it "in part, because of the reasonable likelihood that it will result in fewer lives lost and less destruction of property."[177]

Even if nonviolent actions provoke a violent response in the short term, a disciplined nonviolent movement can work to absorb the violence and reduce its negative impact. In fact, in a number of instances, as observed by civil resistance scholars, violence against nonviolent movements backfires, increasing domestic and international sympathy for the activists and triggering even larger civil resistance mobilization.[178] A nonviolent stance is objectively preferable to violence because it is less costly in economic and emotional terms, both for those engaged in nonviolent resistance as well as those who are its targets and bystanders. For the purposes of the four principles, it is not necessary that the individuals or groups that embrace a nonviolent stance be committed to it in a principled way, as a moral system or philosophy. Some scholars and practitioners of nonviolent civil resistance are apprehensive that nonviolence will be mistaken for "pacifism" and instead stress that it is an alternative means of waging conflict. While it is true that nonviolent practice can be undertaken for pragmatic or strategic purposes— e.g., because it is more likely to succeed than violence, or because the adversary is more powerful in conventional terms—it has been argued that the distinction between principled and pragmatic nonviolence is less pronounced than is sometimes thought. Practitioners of principled nonviolence like Gandhi still need to be pragmatic to achieve their ends. At the same time, pragmatic nonviolent resistance (advocated by Helvey) often has a moral aspect like a desire to avoid the bloodshed or unnecessary casualties that would come from violence. Arguably, either principle-based or pragmatic nonviolent resistance meets the criteria for the general principle of nonviolence, because both respect the right to life. But there is a caveat. A nonviolent movement (like the 1979 Iranian revolution; see Part V of this monograph on "Trojan horses") that employs violence after securing victory without violence would negate the principle of nonviolence.

Synthesis

To pull this framework together now, let's imagine that the two half-grids above (Box 1 and Box 2) are superimposed on one another as follows, with the nature of the rights and implementing mechanisms appropriate to each dimension briefly outlined in the text of the four quadrants (see Box 3). In addition to representing the permeability between the hybrid dimensions of international and domestic law, natural and positive law, the double-sided arrows between the quadrants represent the vectors of activity by means of which the four principles are realized.

Box 3. Analytical interplay between positive human rights law (AB) and natural law rights-advancing movements (DC)

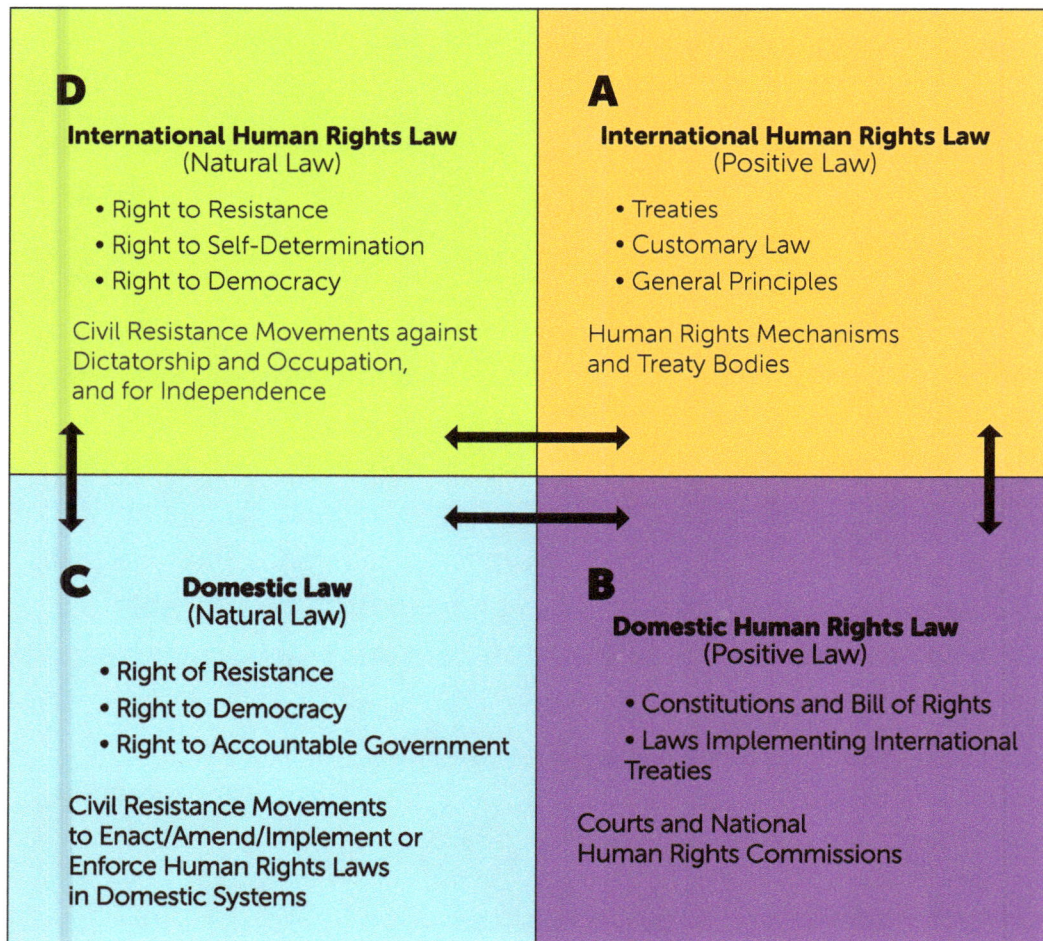

D

International Human Rights Law
(Natural Law)

• Right to Resistance
• Right to Self-Determination
• Right to Democracy

Civil Resistance Movements against Dictatorship and Occupation, and for Independence

A

International Human Rights Law
(Positive Law)

• Treaties
• Customary Law
• General Principles

Human Rights Mechanisms and Treaty Bodies

C

Domestic Law
(Natural Law)

• Right of Resistance
• Right to Democracy
• Right to Accountable Government

Civil Resistance Movements to Enact/Amend/Implement or Enforce Human Rights Laws in Domestic Systems

B

Domestic Human Rights Law
(Positive Law)

• Constitutions and Bill of Rights
• Laws Implementing International Treaties

Courts and National Human Rights Commissions

Quadrant A in the upper-right hand of the diagram represents the positive law of international human rights that protects all human beings; this includes customary law, conventional law, and the institutional human rights mechanisms that enforce them (the UNHRC, treaty bodies, regional human rights courts).

Quadrant B on the lower right represents the domestic legal counterparts to international human rights law; including constitutional and bills of rights provisions that were incorporated into the UDHR; and constitutions and laws implementing international human rights norms after the UDHR and other international human rights law developed. Quadrant B includes also any relevant domestic legal enforcement mechanisms, such as courts, national human rights commissions, executive orders, and administrative processes.

Quadrant C on the lower-left represents natural law, defined as including civil resistance movements that are organized primarily domestically and aimed at realizing human rights in a domestic legal system. Natural law here includes movements aimed both at realizing positive laws that are not being actually enforced and various natural law rights that aspire beyond existing positive law, such as the natural law rights to resist oppression and to accountable government.

Quadrant D designates those civil resistance movements having goals that directly impact the shape of international order, like secession movements or revolutions to end foreign occupation. It also encompasses inchoate or incipient customary international law that is being developed by those movements.

Civil resistance movements that result in democratic revolutions or transitions overlap Quadrants C and D. They are technically considered "internal" under current international law, but their effects can be so dramatic on the international order that in certain respects they may arguably be considered self-determination movements as well (see Part VI).

The bidirectional arrows between the quadrants indicate the vectors of the four principles and some of the potential pathways through which the four dimensions can reciprocally interact with and shape one another.

*   *   *

The second half of this monograph applies the analytical framework (presented in Box 3) to four broad types of real-world scenarios involving civil resistance. Part III examines the first scenario, which concerns how the positive law of human rights may be utilized to protect the rights of individuals engaged in nonviolent civil resistance. Positive human rights law generally protects the rights of individuals, acting both alone and in association. By extension, positive human rights law protects the human rights of those participating in civil resistance movements—e.g., their rights to seek and impart information; to assemble peacefully; to express opinions and engage in free speech; rights to life and freedom from torture and cruel, inhuman and degrading treatment, among various other rights. The international community is now working to clarify the extent of human rights protections of those who are engaged in what is coming to be called "the right to peaceful protest" in international law.

Part IV looks at the second scenario involving civil resistance movements that are aimed at realizing rights recognized in the positive law of international human rights, such as bringing about an end to the use of the death penalty; eliminating discrimination based on race, religion, ethnicity, or gender; or improving women's educational opportunities; ending human trafficking or child soldiering. Civil resistance movements that mainly work within existing state systems may be called "reformist." Using civil resistance, reformist movements may pressure states to implement laws protecting human rights or to better enforce laws they have already implemented. To the extent that they are organized in relation to positive human rights law, civil resistance movements may be regarded as adjunct means to implement or enforce, or cause the state to implement or enforce, positive law through forms of direct actions rather than through standard legal means.

Part V focuses on the third scenario of nonviolent civil resistance campaigns that are not directly organized in relation to positive human rights legal frameworks but either have objectives that are abstract ("dignity" or "freedom") or are broad, self-determination struggles seeking political "regime change" or national or group liberation. These "revolutionary" campaigns would not be included immediately as part of today's human rights project, because such objectives are not explicitly protected in the positive law of human rights. However, the rights often asserted by nonviolent movements—the right to revolution, the right to resist oppression or tyranny—often reflect a sense of natural justice on the part of participants. This monograph argues that such revolutionary movements can nonetheless be seen as human rights movements, if both the ends and the means sought by the activists broadly cohere with the general principles of human rights.

In a hypothetical fourth scenario that this monograph argues can be a realistic and progressive development of international law, Part VI returns to positive law and suggests three ways that people power can be theorized as a source of international human rights law.

Part Two

APPLYING GENERAL PRINCIPLES OF HUMAN RIGHTS TO PEOPLE POWER MOVEMENTS

Chapter III
Positive Human Rights Law Protecting Civil Resistance Movements and their Participants

*T*he first scenario examined here is the "normal" way that international human rights law works: to protect the rights of individuals. Individual and group participants in civil resistance movements are rights-holders and beneficiaries of human rights legal frameworks. They are protected by obligations created by treaties that the state has signed onto and by any human rights norms that have become customary law. In terms of the framework outlined in the first half of this monograph, we are looking here (Box 4) mainly at interactions from positive law (Quadrants A and B) to people power movements operating as natural law (Quadrants C and D).

Box 4. International and domestic positive law (AB) protecting natural law movements (CD)

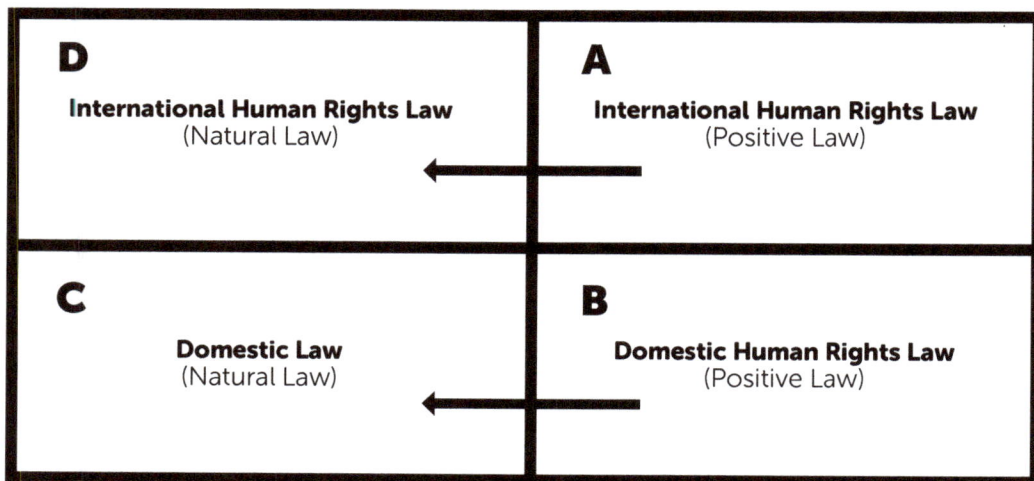

D	**A**
International Human Rights Law (Natural Law)	**International Human Rights Law** (Positive Law)
C	**B**
Domestic Law (Natural Law)	**Domestic Human Rights Law** (Positive Law)

Individual Rights Relevant to Nonviolent Civil Resistance

People power movements can assert a broad array of rights, but this part focusses on the rights that protect individuals engaged in public demonstrations, marches, occupations, sit-ins, or related actions that have the purpose of expressing views, opinions, dissatisfactions, and dissent. Although nonviolent civil resistance can take myriad forms, these are the most visible, and most risky for participants as they can easily be exposed to state repression. The human rights that participants in a movement can invoke and exercise while waging their nonviolent struggle are mostly found in the ICCPR and include the following:

Collective rights
- Article 1 (self-determination).

Expressive and associational rights
- Article 18 (freedom of thought, conscience and religion);
- Article 19 (freedom of opinion and expression);
- Article 21 (freedom of peaceful assembly);
- Article 22 (freedom of association);
- Article 25 (right to political participation).

Bodily integrity rights
- Article 6 (right to life)
- Article 7 (freedom from torture; cruel, inhuman and degrading treatment);
- Article 9 (liberty and security; freedom from arbitrary arrest and detention);
- Article 10 (dignity).[179]

Until recently, the scope of many of the expressive and associational rights involved in peaceful protest were not very clear. First, the provisions in the ICCPR providing for the rights of peaceful assembly, association, and expression contain "clawback" clauses permitting states to limit those rights under certain (vague) circumstances, such as to ensure *ordre public* or protect "morals" or "the rights of others."[180] To what extent exactly can the relevant rights be limited, and for how long, exactly? Despite need for clarification, the Human Rights Committee (HRC)—the treaty body entrusted with enforcing the

ICCPR and overseeing state party compliance with the treaty—has thus far not issued General Comments on either Article 21 (peaceful assembly) or Article 22 (freedom of association), leaving clarification of these rights and the circumstances under which they can be legitimately curtailed to the UNHRC and its special procedures.[181]

Second, except for freedom of thought, conscience, and religion in Article 18, all of the rights relevant to the right of peaceful protest may be derogated from under circumstances of public emergency. This means that when a state is confronted with a public emergency (such as a terrorist attack), it may lawfully violate certain expressive and associational human rights for a delimited period of time, so long as the state informs the Secretary-General of the UN of its actions.[182]

As noted in the introduction, in view of the increasing use of peaceful protest (that coincides, as observed by scholars, with an extraordinary growth of nonviolent movements) around the world, the UNHRC has expressed concern at the violence that states are using to respond to public demonstrations. In early 2014, the UNHRC invited the Office of the High Commissioner for Human Rights to organize a seminar on "effective measures and best practices to ensure the promotion and protection of human rights in the context of peaceful protests."[183] A few months later, the UNHRC called on member states, *inter alia*, "to promote a safe and enabling environment for individuals and groups to exercise their rights to freedom of peaceful assembly, of expression and of association;" and to ensure that these rights are protected in domestic legislation and effectively implemented.[184] The results of these efforts have been the recognition and clarification of the right to peaceful protest and of the corresponding duty of the state to properly "manage" public demonstrations.

The Right of Peaceful Protest

The "right to protest" is the term increasingly being used by the international community in response to the upwelling of nonviolent protest. Recognized in the Commentary to the DHRD, the term designates the group of rights, enumerated above, that may be implicated during assemblies or protests. The right to peaceful protest is understood as an "amalgamated" right encompassing most of these rights, with the exception of self-determination. In legal terms, the amalgamated nature of the right to peaceful protest means that, in the contest of adjudicating disputes regarding peaceful protests, discrete rights—like the right to peaceful assembly—must be interpreted in light of the other relevant rights such as freedom of expression.

An example of this is found in a case *Stankov v. Bulgaria*, decided by the European Court of Human Rights (ECtHR) in 2001. *Stankov* involved an organization called the United Macedonian Organization Ilinden, a Macedonian independence and cultural identity organization, and their former chairman Boris Stankov (Ilinden).[185] A dispute arose with the state of Bulgaria over repeated denials of Ilinden's requests to hold counter-demonstrations concurrent with official ceremonies marking historical events particularly around the gravesite of the historic revolutionary Yane Ivanov Sandanski. Officially, Sandanski was recognized as a Bulgarian hero, but Ilinden wished to express an alternative view that he was in reality "a Macedonian fighter for the national independence of Macedonia from Turkish rule and against the Bulgarian oppressors."

Ilinden complained that even though their requests to hold a rally were not denied, members were only allowed to approach Sandanski's grave if they left behind their signs and placards and made no speeches graveside. The Bulgarian government argued that imposing these terms on the demonstration struck "a fair balance" between rights and their limitation (para. 108). The ECtHR rejected Bulgaria's argument and held that, though permitted physically to assemble, Ilinden members were denied the right to express their dissenting opinions. The court further held that it should have been possible for the official celebration and Ilinden's counter-celebration to have been held concurrently or in short succession (para. 109). Accordingly, the ECtHR ruled in favor of Ilinden. When it comes to public demonstrations, the right to peaceful assembly and the right to expression have to be interpreted in light of one another.

The Joint Report Recommendations on Peaceful Assemblies

Recently, the UNHRC has undertaken to clarify how the state should behave when confronted with peaceful protest. In the same resolution in which it called on states to provide a safe and enabling environment, the UNHRC tasked the special rapporteur on the rights to freedom of peaceful assembly and of association and the special rapporteur on extrajudicial, summary or arbitrary executions to produce a report compiling "practical recommendations" for the proper management of assemblies.[186] The Joint Report was presented to the UNHRC in March 2016. The mandate-holders were not limited to peaceful assemblies but told to address all assemblies, whether peaceful or not.[187] The Joint Report provides valuable guidance to those organizing public demonstrations as part of civil resistance movements. In drawing up the guidelines, the special rapporteurs relied heavily on the jurisprudence of the ECtHR, which has developed significant case law involving association, peaceful assembly, and related rights.

The Joint Report is merely soft law at this point, meaning that it is not directly binding on states. Soft law can also evolve into more enforceable rights or obligations as it influences state practice and gives rise to new customary norms. The most immediate way the Joint Report could be translated into hard law is through being integrated into the Universal Periodic Review (UPR) process at the UN.

The Report usefully clarifies the scope of the limitations that may be imposed on peaceful assembly and association in accordance with the clawback provisions of the ICCPR. The specificity of its recommendations mean that its guidance will be easy for states to apply. It is particularly helpful because it clarifies the permissible restrictions that may be imposed on assemblies in the name of governmental interests such as national security or public safety. The following are some of the important highlights of the document.

The Report states that a presumption exists in favor of peaceful assembly, and "peaceful" should be interpreted broadly (para. 18). There exists an "inalienable right" to peaceful assembly (para. 18). The Report defines "assemblies" in a broad and comprehensive sense that encompasses "long-term demonstrations," "extended sit-ins," and "'occupy'-style manifestations" (para. 10).[188]

States have the obligation to facilitate the right to peaceful assembly, and prior authorization requirements should be reasonable. Assemblies should only be subject to prior authorization by governmental authorities where the objective is to better enable the government to "facilitate exercise of the right, to take measures to protect public safety and/or public order and to protect the rights and freedoms of others" (para. 21). Any laws restricting assemblies must be unambiguously drafted and meet standards related to legality, necessity, and proportionality. For example, blanket bans are "intrinsically disproportionate" (para. 30), and thus impermissible. In invoking national security or public order, a state cannot refer generally to the security situation; it must demonstrate the specific nature of the threat and the risk posed (para. 31). The content of an assembly's message can only be restricted if it "advocates national, racial or religious hatred that constitutes incitement to discrimination, hostility or violence" (para. 33). Spontaneous assemblies should be exempt from prior authorization requirements altogether (para. 23).

The obligation upon the state to facilitate the right of peaceful assembles requires states to develop a framework that complies with international standards to respect and protect the rights of participants, monitors, and bystanders (para. 50). "Laws governing State conduct in relation to assemblies should be drafted unambiguously" and should also meet legality, necessity and proportionality tests (para. 36(a)). The principle of legality requires the state to develop a legal framework that "restrict[s] the use of weapons and tactics during assemblies, including protests, and include[s] a formal approval and deployment process for weaponry and equipment" (para. 51). There must be a "clear command structure" among police or security officers to minimize risk of violence, as well as a record of all decisions made (para. 65). "States should prohibit by law any interference with the recording of an assembly" (para. 72(d)).

The Joint Report sets out detailed guidelines for the use of force, establishing objective criteria for determining when the state is justified in using violence against protesters. In accordance with principles of legality, precaution, necessity, proportionality and accountability (para. 50), the state should develop a domestic legal framework guiding law enforcement and security forces on the use of force. If the call for violence is coming from one or a small group of individuals, the state should try to isolate such individuals and allow the rest of the assembly to occur (para. 61). Full dispersal is only warranted in rare circumstances. The Joint Report sets out two exceptions that allow for dispersal when other, less-intrusive means have failed: 1) where participants are inciting "discrimination, hostility or violence," in contravention of Art. 20 of the ICCPR (para. 52);[189] and 2) "where an assembly prevents access to essential services, such as blocking the emergency entrance to a hospital, or where interference with traffic or the economy is serious and sustained, for example, where a major highway is blocked for days .." (para. 62). But firing indiscriminately into a crowd is not permissible (para. 60), and automatic weapons are not to be used under any circumstances (para. 67(e)).

While the right to peaceful assembly may be "forfeit[ed]" by an individual who elects to use violence (para. 9), even violent individuals who have forfeited their right to peaceful assembly are still protected by all other human rights (para. 9), including the rights to life and freedom from torture and mistreatment.

From Peaceful Assembly to People Power

The Joint Report lays an important foundation in validating nonviolent civil resistance and creating a space for it in international law, underscoring that individuals and groups of individuals have an "inalienable right" to participate in peaceful assemblies. The recommendations in the Report incentivize nonviolent resistance and maintenance of nonviolent discipline by emphasizing that this right is inalienable so long as protesters remain peaceful. Only individuals who become violent "forfeit their right to peaceful assembly" (para. 9). The Joint Report also establishes that states have an affirmative duty, not just to permit peaceful assemblies to take place but to facilitate the right of peaceful assembly by implementing the report's recommendations (II, D). The broad definition of assembly in the Joint Report in principle ensures that the right to public protest may be exercised to a wide extent. If followed, the recommendations in the Report would obligate states to adopt a nonviolent policy stance and respond to disciplined nonviolent campaigns with reciprocal nonviolent discipline on the part of state agents (e.g., security forces), taking only necessary and proportional actions in response to any violence that might occur. While it remains to be seen to what extent these recommendations are incorporated into the UPR process at the UN and solidified as customary norms, the Joint Report is a useful document for civil resisters to become familiar with.

Despite important steps in clarifying the law on peaceful assembly, the Joint Report falls short of providing a comprehensive analytical framework for situating nonviolent civil resistance in international human rights law. Nonviolent civil resistance may involve a wide variety of extra-legal or extra-institutional actions, not all of which are large-scale assemblies in public places, and different legal norms may apply to different tactics.[190] The premise of the Report is that "the ability to assemble and act collectively is vital to democratic, economic, social and personal development, to the expression of ideas and to fostering engaged citizenry" (para. 5), even though not all states in the international community are committed to fostering citizen engagement and democratic development. The Report draws no distinction between assemblies that have the purpose of expressing dissenting views on specific policies in a democratic marketplace of ideas and those that bring together individuals who are demanding more radical and system-wide change, up to and including the fall of the government. It thus provides no guidance as to the obligations of the state or international community at crucial moments of an escalating nonviolent struggle.

Using Human Rights Mechanisms

To what extent are the reporting and individual complaint procedures available through the international human rights legal mechanism useful to participants in civil resistance movements in realizing their right to peaceful protest and other human rights relevant to nonviolent civil resistance? As yet, the HRC has not been significantly utilized to support the right of peaceful assembly. Moreover, the full complaint process before treaty bodies is slow and it may take years for a decision to be rendered. Treaty bodies would not be of much use in responding immediately, for example, when state security forces use disproportionate force against nonviolent activists engaged in nonviolent protest. During mobilization of a mass movement, events on the ground may change rapidly, making the drawn-out legal processes involving international treaty bodies impractical. In a single night, the police may use undue force to clear a site where demonstrators have congregated, but it may take days or weeks for lawyers to file a complaint and months—or even years—before the treaty body renders a final judgment. Consideration should be given to the likely value-added of appeal to such mechanisms above the "naming and shaming" that human rights organizations may provide.

Precautionary Measures

In some regions of the world, swifter legal results may be obtained through the use of "precautionary measures," such as are available in the Inter-American and European human rights regional frameworks and from some treaty bodies. For example, an individual or group confronted with grave and immediate harm can ask the Inter-American Commission of Human Rights (IACHR) to direct an urgent request to a member state to take "injunctive measures."[191] Precautionary measures may protect groups as well as persons, and they are indicated when an action or omission may have a "grave impact" on a protected right or pending decision: when the "risk or threat... is imminent" and would cause "irreparable harm," defined as "injury to rights which, due to their nature, would not be susceptible to reparation, restoration or adequate compensation."[192] Precautionary measures can be granted in a matter of weeks,[193] soon enough, for example, to order that a woman carrying an unviable fetus be granted the medical procedures necessary to save her life in a country where abortion is illegal[194] or, theoretically, quick enough to push against or put a country on notice that international law is being violated by the expected ban on peaceful protests or other draconian measures designed to punish activists. Apart from the Inter-American regional human rights system, most human rights mechanisms issuing precautionary measures do not make them public, so it is difficult to know how widely used or effective they are.[195] Nevertheless, depending on whether the particular state has ratified a relevant human rights treaty, treaty body and regional human rights mechanisms may be available and can carry weight for regimes that care about their international reputation. Treaty bodies that issue precautionary measures include the HRC, the Committee Against Torture, the Committee on the Elimination of All Forms of Discrimination Against Women, and the Committee on the Elimination of Racial Discrimination, among others. Nonviolent activists may want to familiarize themselves with the precautionary measures that may be available to them.

If movements continue to use available international human rights mechanisms over time, it is possible that this may help to create a more propitious legal climate inside the country for peaceful protest, but this is not guaranteed. Appeal to regional human rights courts or domestic constitutional courts, as some of the examples below will show, may be most efficacious.

Human Rights Committee: Belarus

One exception to the non-use of the treaty body mechanisms is the case of Belarus. Of 31 Views adopted by the HRC involving Article 21, 25 of them involved Belarus.[196] The great majority of those occurred between 2006 and 2010, when elections widely perceived to be fraudulent brought large numbers of Belarussians out into the streets. The beneficiary of the elections, President Aleksander Lukashenko, vowed that his country would not fall victim to another "color revolution" and cracked down harshly on political demonstrations, more often with fines and jail terms than physical violence, though violence did occur. In view of this repression, it cannot be said that utilization of the human rights mechanisms by Belarussian activists led to any long-term success in creating a more open climate for protest. However, use of these mechanisms indicates the sophistication of Belarussian activists in their strategic planning and repression management. Activists changed tactics, organizing smaller and swifter political demonstrations (flash mobs) or silent demonstrations and turned more often to small-scale "social protests" aimed at contesting housing projects or getting companies to pay arrears or resisting trade regulations. Such social protests have often been successful and faced few if no reprisals from the government.[197]

Amparo Actions: Guatemala

Available in most Latin American countries is a constitutional action called the writ of *amparo* that can be used to enforce constitutional rights. This was used effectively to support mass-based nonviolent demonstrations in Guatemala in 2015. After revelations about serious corruption by a high-level Guatemalan official were made public in mid-April 2015, several ordinary people in Guatemala created a Facebook page calling for a protest to take place on April 25. When 10,000 people indicated they would show up, organizers began to think seriously about how to provide safety and maintain a nonviolent atmosphere around their protest. In addition to deciding to congregate in one place rather than march and not to have leaders or speakers that would seem affiliated with a political party, the organizers worked with a lawyer who initiated an *amparo* action on their behalf at the *Corte de Constitucionalidad* (Constitutional Court). This is a court that is designed to review laws or lower court rulings to make sure that the constitution is correctly interpreted and applied. Article 33 of Guatemala's Constitution protects the right of assembly and demonstration or protest (*manifestacion*). In addition to asking the Court to enforce that right, the organizers also asked the Court to enforce Article 2 of the Constitution, which provides that the State of Guatemala has the duty "to guarantee to the inhabitants of the Republic the life, the freedom, the justice, the security, the peace, and the integral development of the person."

The Constitutional Court granted their petition, ordering the president to direct the *Ministro de Gobernación* (Ministry of the Interior) to provide security through the police force and made the president personally responsible for the security of all protesters present. The Court also ordered municipal firefighters to have ambulances present to provide medical assistance, and it advised the Human Rights Ombudsman office to provide assistance and ensure that human rights would be guarded. A series of successful nonviolent protests against what was perceived as a highly corrupt ruling class led first to the resignation of the vice-president and government ministers and then eventually brought about the resignation of President Otto Perez Molina in

September 2015.[198]

Hong Kong

In the heat of the moment, creative methods may be found to assert human rights protected by relevant treaties. After protesters in Hong Kong learned that police were planning to evacuate their encampments, they warned the police to respect human rights with the following announcement:

Source: Independent Thinking Blog, via Creative Commons.

Risk of Backlash

Those who are part of a nonviolent campaign must also consider risk of using international human rights mechanisms since there are few if any protections to prevent the state from retaliating against activists who appeal to outside institutions.

With recalcitrant governments, use of human rights mechanisms may provoke backlash in the form of denunciation of human rights treaties. Venezuelan citizen Raul Dias Pena won a case against Venezuela in 2012 before the Inter-American Court of Human Rights (IACtHR) in relation to illegal treatment he received after being arrested in connection with bombings that occurred in diplomatic properties of Colombia and Spain.[199] Though Pena was not a human rights defender and the case does not seem to be related to any organized protests,[200] the decision of the IACtHR and its order to pay reparations to Pena prompted Venezuela to denounce the American Convention for Human Rights—the treaty giving the IACtHR jurisdiction over Venezuela[201]—and to accuse the court of being an imperialist tool of the US government. As a result of Venezuela's denunciation of the regional human rights treaty, human rights defenders in Venezuela turned their sights to the treaty bodies and UPR process at the UN.[202]

While use of human rights legal mechanisms by activists may carry a risk of a negative backlash, it may at the same time underscore that the movement is respecting the principle of nonviolence and seeking to exercise the human rights of expression and peaceful assembly. This in turn may encourage wider participation and enhance popular support, thus building strength and momentum for the movement in the long term. The reputational costs for a government might be especially severe if the movement's campaigns are ongoing and unlikely to dissipate quickly, presenting the governmental authorities with a particularly difficult dilemma.

To conclude discussion of the first scenario, Box 4 designates the "normal" way international human rights law is supposed to work. Protections flow from the positive law to individuals and groups via the appropriate mechanisms and, in principle, the law protects the right to engage in nonviolent demonstrations and assemblies. International human rights law is still evolving a legal framework that would protect the full range of nonviolent civil resistance activities. Because of the weakness of international human rights mechanisms, except in the Latin American and European regions, activists in non-authoritarian countries may find that domestic law provides a higher degree of protection. Nevertheless, seeking the protection of the human rights mechanisms enumerated and described above may help legitimate nonviolent protest, domestically and internationally.

Chapter IV
Realizing the Positive Law of Human Rights

*T*he second scenario in which we can apply the framework of general principles is when civil resistance movements utilize or refer to international or domestic human rights legal frameworks. This happens because movements, often for strategic and utilitarian reasons, recognize and want to publicly acknowledge the affinity between their demands and the rights they are accorded in positive human rights law.

Box 5. Effects of civil resistance movements utilizing or referring to human rights frameworks

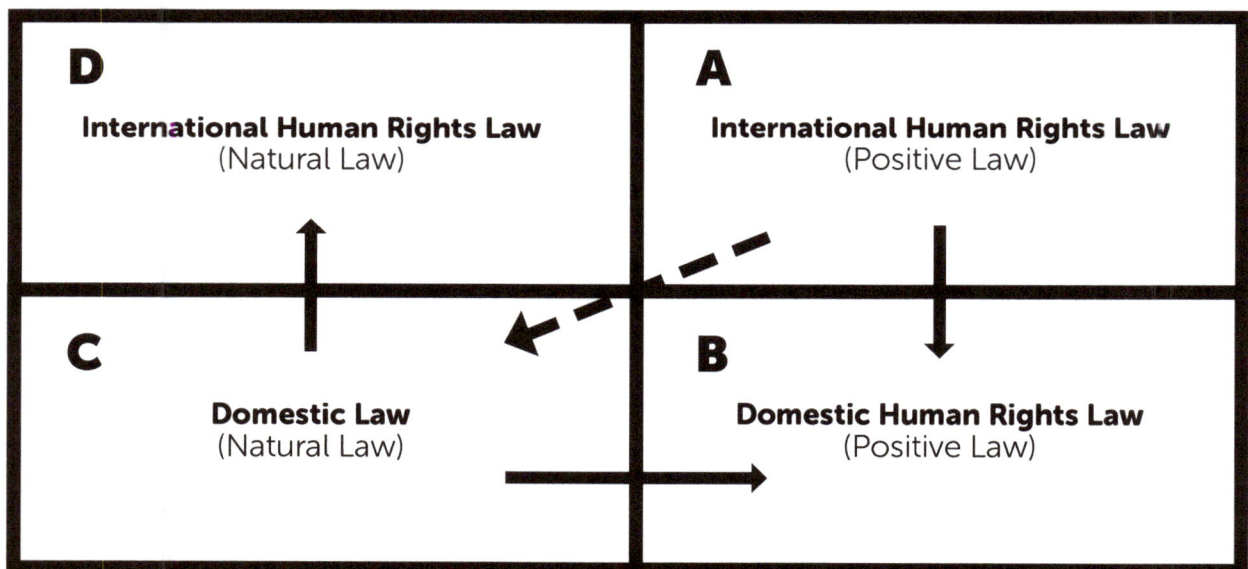

D	A
International Human Rights Law (Natural Law)	**International Human Rights Law** (Positive Law)
C	B
Domestic Law (Natural Law)	**Domestic Human Rights Law** (Positive Law)

When this occurs, a wide variety of effects can ensue (see Box 5). After a state has engaged with international human rights positive law to the extent of signing or ratifying a treaty or passing implementing legislation (line A to B), civil resisters may be aware of such developments (dotted line A to C) and may organize people power movements to press for more effective implementation of the law, or for the government to institute a related specific policy or institutional change (line C to B). Here natural law refers to people power movements organized to enhance the workings of positive law. Movements organized in such ways have been termed "rightful resistance," because they work with, rather than against, positive law.[203]

n such cases, civil resistance may function as a kind of adjunct to legal enforcement mechanisms, helping to give them effect. In more democratic contexts, civil resistance may work with positive law but ultimately aim beyond it.[204] With recalcitrant states like China or Saudi Arabia, the main engagement that a domestic campaign or a movement might have with human rights legal frameworks is to organize domestic protests around the UPR process at the UN. Finally, in some cases, broad appeal to a foundational treaty like the ICCPR can initially begin with incremental reformist steps but culminate years later in revolutionary outcomes (line C to D) that seek to realize natural law rights like democracy or self-determination. Perhaps the most important and most well-known use by movements of treaty law resulted in the anti-communist revolutions in Central and Eastern Europe, as explained below.

Appeal to Treaties and Treaty Bodies

The simplest and most straightforward way for civil resistance movements to appeal to human rights legal frameworks is basically to remind states of their treaty obligations. Where a nonviolent movement is overtly focused on a right clearly defined in an applicable human rights treaty, it can be regarded as a human rights movement, even though the target of the campaign may reject the claim.

The Umbrella Movement

The Umbrella Movement in Hong Kong that began in September 2014 is an example of a relatively focused campaign that appealed to a specific right (political participation) protected in an applicable treaty (the ICCPR). Opposing the Chinese government's desire to retain the power to nominate candidates for Hong Kong's highest leadership position (the chief executive), protesters demanded that Hong Kong residents should have the right to stand for election as well as the right to choose their own candidates.[205] During those demonstrations, Occupy Central invoked the ICCPR repeatedly, e.g., tweeting on June 30, "Universal suffrage is a basic political right (ICCPR Art.25) that must be realized IMMEDIATELY. BasicLaw Art39: #HongKong is subject to ICCPR."

Source: Twitter user @CCPR_Centre, October 23, 2014.

China has signed but never ratified the ICCPR.[206] The reason the ICCPR applies to Hong Kong even though Hong Kong is not a state and therefore not a state party to the ICCPR, is that the ICCPR had applied to Hong Kong during its time as a British Commonwealth country. In the legally binding international treaty China signed with Great Britain effecting the transfer of Hong Kong's sovereignty, it was stipulated that the ICCPR would continue to apply to Hong Kong.[207] This was also written into the Hong Kong Basic Law.

Not only have demonstrators appealed to the ICCPR, but the HRC has issued views on the substance of the demands regarding political participation rights. Since 1999, the periodic reports required by the ICCPR have been submitted by the Hong Kong Special Administrative Region of the People's Republic of China, giving the HRC the opportunity to render its legal opinion about the extent of the ICCPR's application in Hong Kong. Despite the slowness of their official processes, human rights treaty bodies or other legal mechanisms can sometimes make quasi-legal expressions of support in a timely fashion. During the course of the Umbrella Movement in Hong Kong, the HRC has backed up protesters' demands, and it pronounced in October 2014, at the height of the demonstrations, that the Hong Kong authorities had no right to limit political participation rights.[208]

Source: Twitter user @CCPR_Centre, October 23, 2014.

China rejected the idea that the treaty was "a measure for Hong Kong's political reform;"[209] however, in responding to the HRC, it implicitly acknowledged that the treaty did in fact apply to Hong Kong.[210]

Actions Organized around Human Rights Legal Frameworks

Another way that nonviolent actors can interact with human rights positive law is by organizing activities around important events transpiring in human rights-related legal mechanisms. For example, because of the new structure of the UNHRC, even countries that have not signed the ICCPR, like China, will have their human rights record reviewed every four years under the UPR process. States under review submit an official report, and if permitted, civil society groups from the countries under review submit unofficial "shadow" reports. The UNHRC then prepares a summary document that is used as the basis for the review session. This review session is a public forum where the state under review appears and receives recommendations from the other UN member states. Approximately four months later, the state under review appears again in a public forum for what is known as an adoption session, in which the state formally indicates whether it will accept or reject the recommendations. For a few days every four years, the UPR review shines a spotlight on a state's human rights laws and policies. Human rights defenders and civil society groups have organized nonviolent actions coinciding with the UPR process.

China

China's UPR review and its uncontested accession to a seat on the UNHRC gave Chinese activists a chance to rally around the UN process in 2013. Unlike most countries in the world, China does not let CSOs participate in the UPR, though the shadow reports filed by such organizations are an important source of information about the actual human rights record in the country under review. Even so, Chinese activists mobilized around the UPR process and organized numerous actions around the country, culminating in a sit-in at the Ministry of Foreign Affairs in June. Chinese officials had declined numerous freedom of information requests and ultimately declared that the UPR process was a matter of state security. During the UPR review itself, human rights organizations in China made relevant announcements, and international Chinese human rights activists staged demonstrations in Geneva, where the UPR takes place.[211]

Egypt

When the Egyptian government was undergoing its UPR review in 2010, 16 human rights CSOs formed a coalition in order to present the UNHRC with an alternative to the official report submitted by the government. Much of the work that the coalition engaged in involved legal activities such as writing and submitting the report, and then lobbying state parties sitting on the UNHRC to get them to adopt particular recommendations, which they did. But the coalition also utilized the Egyptian media to create greater public interest in the proceedings.[212] As a result of coalition efforts, independent newspapers in Egypt ran front-page coverage of the UPR process and publicized the coalition's alternative report.[213] Because of the perceived importance of the UPR in determining a state's international legitimacy, the Egyptian government took the process seriously. A representative for the coalition noted, "The [Egyptian] news, *Al Ahram*—even government papers gave us space. There is an increasing awareness in society."[214] The coalition also organized a "100-day campaign" in Egypt between February 19, the last day of the UNHRC session during which Egypt had been reviewed,[215] and June 6, 2010, a few days before the adoption session on June 11, 2010.[216] During this campaign, the civic coalition closely monitored the government's actions and compared them to the promises made during the review session. At the adoption session in Geneva, the Egyptian government had arranged for "friendly" nations such as Algeria and Saudi Arabia to vouch for Egypt's human rights commitment. By happenstance, on the day of the adoption session, Egyptian police tortured and killed a young man named Khaled Saeed in Alexandria, even while a delegation from the Egyptian government was in Geneva to adopt recommendations from its UPR review. This irony prompted the independent newspaper *Al Shorouk* to pen a sarcastic headline: "After hours from the Alexandria incident, Arab states praise Egypt's human rights report!"[217] Another independent newspaper then organized a seminar with members from the coalition to learn more about the UPR process.[218]

Pressuring States to Enforce Domestic Law Reflecting, or Implemented to Fulfill, International Human Rights Obligations

Civil resistance movements can also be fairly characterized as human rights movements and their campaigns as human rights campaigns if they aim at pressuring a national government to pass legislation implementing international human rights obligations, or to better enforce domestic laws adopted to fulfill such obligations. This is a presumption that can be rebutted if, in their activities, the movements violate the general principles identified earlier.

In such cases, civil resistance may be part of a multipronged strategy, since implementation of international law is an inherently legal process that requires technical legal expertise. For example, Costa Rica ratified CEDAW in 1984. Because it had taken four years of intense advocacy to achieve ratification after Costa Rica signed CEDAW in 1980, domestic supporters of the treaty were eager to pass implementing legislation as soon as the ratification occurred and hold the newly elected President Oscar Arias to his campaign promise that his government would have "the soul of a woman."[219] A coalition of civil society actors developed a multipronged strategy including town hall meetings, "cultural fairs," interviews with press and media, and a 5,000 woman march to the legislative assembly.[220] At the end of the campaign, the coalition commissioned a public opinion survey showing that a majority approved of the implementing legislation. It eventually became law in 1990.[221]

Another appeal to human rights treaties occurred in Jordan in the 1990s, with a grassroots, largely women-led, campaign to end impunity for honor killings. The specific targets of the campaign were two provisions in the Jordanian penal code that made it nearly impossible to prosecute perpetrators of honor killings. Art. 98 stated, "Any person who commits a crime in a fit of fury caused by an unlawful and dangerous act on the part of the victim benefits from a reduction in penalty." Art. 340 contained two objectionable provisions: "He who discovers his wife or one of his female relatives committing adultery (with a man) and kills, wounds, or injures one or both of them, is exempted from any penalty"; and "He who discovers his wife, or one of his female relatives with another in an adulterous situation, and kills, wounds or injures one or both of them, benefits from a reduction in penalty."[222]

The campaign was launched with a press conference where organizers read a petition asserting "the right of each Jordanian to live in peace and harmony based on respect for human dignity, individual rights, justice, security, fair trial and defence." They also stated that honor killings "contradict Islamic law (Sharia), the Constitution and CEDAW."[223] The appeal to CEDAW in the petition was meaningful since Jordan had ratified it on July 1, 1992. Consisting of petitions, rallies and marches, the campaign against the honor killing laws succeeded in raising consciousness and garnering support for repeal of the laws, although the short-term political result was only a disingenuous amendment of Art. 340 to allow it to apply to women perpetrators, thus making the law "non-discriminatory."

From Positive Law to Natural Law

In some cases, activism by civil society groups that initially aims at inducing states to fulfill their obligations under the positive law of international human rights may sow the seeds for later, large-scale civil resistance campaigns pursuing goals that exceed the positive law and assert natural law rights, such as the right to peaceful resistance or the right to self-determination. Instead of seeking reform of a legal or political system, the movement is seeking its wholesale overhaul. The most well-known example of how appeals to positive law culminated in natural law demands occurred in the former Soviet Union after the "Final Act" of the Conference on Security and Cooperation in Europe, signed by the Western countries and the Soviet Union, together with its Eastern and Central European communist allies in 1975.

The Helsinki Effect

Part of the "Final Act" was the so-called "Third Basket," which came to be known as the "Helsinki Accords." In the Accords, countries of the Western Bloc recognized the inviolability of the Soviet Union's borders in exchange for countries of the eastern bloc committing themselves to respect "human rights and fundamental freedoms, including freedom of thought, conscience, religion, or belief, for all without distinction as to race, sex, language or religion."[224] Though technically non-binding, the Accords contained references to the International Covenants that eventually gave them teeth. In what appears in retrospect to have been a political miscalculation, the Soviet and East European negotiators of the Final Act thought that the human rights provisions in the ICCPR and ICESCR were paper tigers because of the deep "escape clauses" in the form of the clawback provisions in certain of the Articles.[225] So confident of this were they that they even accelerated the ratification process. The Soviet Union ratified both treaties on October 16, 1973, near the beginning of the drafting process for the Helsinki Final Act. Then-Czechoslovakia acceded to the ICCPR in 1976, bringing the treaty into force.[226] Despite this misperception, in the late 1970s and throughout the 1980s, civic campaigns challenging the communist authorities in Poland, Czechoslovakia, and the Soviet Union coalesced around the human rights provisions included in the Accords. Soon after their adoption in 1975, physicist Yuri Orlov and a group of other dissidents in Moscow founded a civil society monitoring organization—the Moscow Helsinki Watch. Similar Helsinki monitoring groups and organizations were soon formed in Soviet bloc states; in Czechoslovakia, Charter 77 was created in 1977, in Poland, the Movement for the Defense of Human and Civic Rights was created in 1977 and the Helsinki Committee in 1982. Informal Helsinki human rights groups were also formed in Soviet Union republics.[227]

The creation of human rights CSOs after the Helsinki Accords over time played a pivotal role in broadening civic space and thus enabling larger mobilization and nonviolent resistance in communist countries. Soviet and East European dissidents were able to appeal to the broad civil and political rights provisions in the ICCPR and Helsinki Accords and to ramp up international pressure, further delegitimizing the actions of the communist regimes. The ICCPR and ICESCR were especially helpful to dissidents in countries lacking a liberal constitution.[228]

The work inspired by the Helsinki Accords and ICCPR human rights provisions catalyzed revolutionary movements in many Soviet bloc countries that eventually threw off Soviet domination and instituted democratic reforms. Thomas, for example, credits the mobilization of human rights organizations, along with a change in the diplomatic agenda, as being an impetus for the revolutions in 1989 that brought an end to the Soviet Union.[229]

Although in a much shorter timeframe, something similar happened in Egypt. Partly because of the media coverage generated by the 100-day campaign that covered the human rights-related actions of the Egyptian government during crucial period of the UPR, the horrific death of Khaled Saeed "sparked unprecedented popular outrage"[230] and was an important prelude to the Tahrir Square uprising in January 2011. A Facebook page dedicated to his memory—"We are all Khaled Saeed"—garnered 180,000 followers in just one month.[231] Although challenging to quantify how much it ultimately contributed to the uprising, the attention that the UPR-centered civic campaign brought to the Egyptian government's appalling human rights record undeniably played a role in raising anti-regime feeling. It also helped activists hone their mobilization skills, and created relationships among various civic groups.

Chapter V
Realizing the Natural Law of Human Rights

When civil resistance movements appeal to international human rights treaties or mechanisms to realize their objectives or to pressure a state to meet its obligations under international law, it seems self-evident that they are engaged in a collective praxis aimed at realizing human rights. However, not all nonviolent movements want, or are able, to make use of these mechanisms. Participants may be citizens whose states have not ratified relevant human rights treaties. They may not have access to lawyers or other persons knowledgeable about human rights mechanisms. Events on the ground may be moving too rapidly for recourse to such mechanisms to make sense.

Furthermore, as the example of the Helsinki Accords indicates, appeal to human rights treaties may culminate in revolutionary civil resistance movements. Such movements have as their stated objectives either a change in government, an end to foreign occupation, or the creation of a new state. None of these are protected rights in positive human rights law, even though such objectives seem to loosely correspond with the human rights "ends" of freedom, peace, and justice. Some scholars consider such revolutionary movements as something quite different from human rights movements— as citizenship efforts to (re)constitute a state or replace its government, not necessarily to advance human rights *per se*. To Moyn, a human rights movement by definition does not work through domestic law, because international human rights presupposes a legal system that is global in nature. But since human rights activists have never sought or predicted the withering away of states but rather their betterment, it is more accurate to say that the aim of the human rights project is to realize rights in the national context, with regional and international mechanisms acting as a backstop.

This monograph does not see a necessary antithesis between human rights movements and revolutionary movements. Solidarity was an independence movement in a sense that its long-term goal was to free the Polish state from Soviet subjugation. But Solidarity activists knew that Poland could never be truly independent if Poles themselves did not win and enjoy their civic, political and economic rights through a liberated state structure. Political scientist and former member of Solidarity, Jan Kubik has remarked, "There is an idea that Solidarity was a 'nationalist movement'—it was in reality about something much more profound. It was about dignity, it was about freedom..." However, because such revolutionary ends as independence or democracy exceed the formal parameters of positive human rights law, it is necessary to turn back here to natural law, in order to theorize precisely how revolutionary movements may be seen as human rights movements. It will be recalled that natural law is being redefined in this monograph to mean the *jurisgenesis* of civil resistance movements acting in accordance with the general principles of human rights.

In the third scenario (see Box 6), this monograph considers people power movements that are engaged in realizing the natural law of human rights.

Box 6. Visualization of civil resistance movements realizing the natural law of human rights

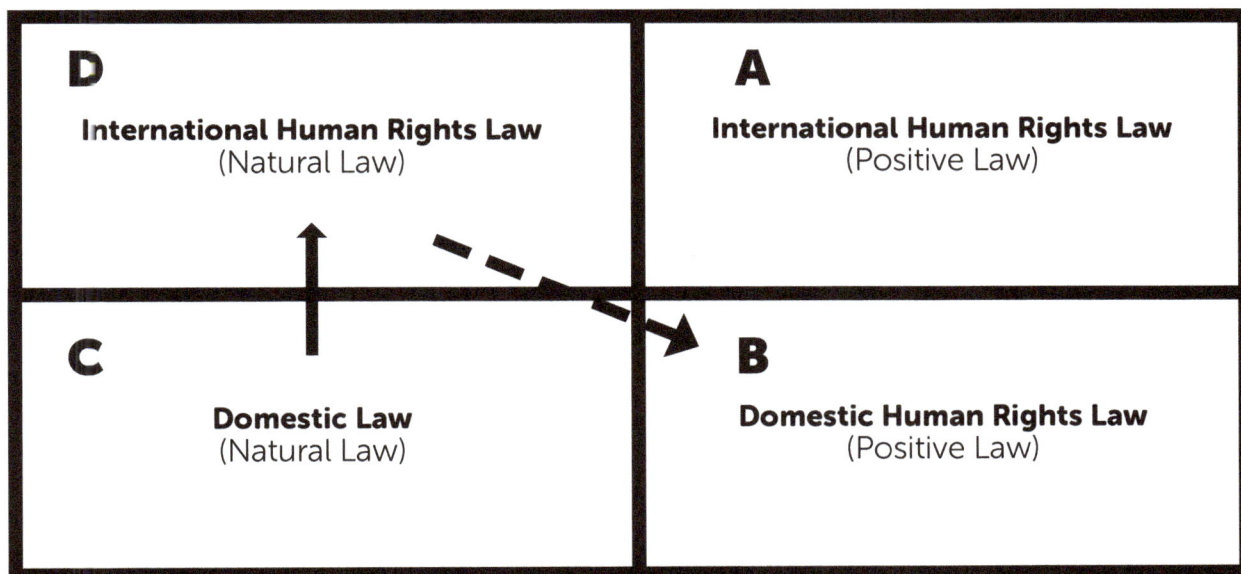

D	A
International Human Rights Law (Natural Law)	**International Human Rights Law** (Positive Law)
C	B
Domestic Law (Natural Law)	**Domestic Human Rights Law** (Positive Law)

The scenario of civil resistance movements realizing the natural law of human rights can be visualized by an arrow moving from Quadrant C to Quadrant D, and then perhaps another arrow returning to Quadrant B. The starting location of Quadrant C signifies that a "maximalist" or revolutionary people power movement is almost always organized within the political and physical confines of an existing nation-state. The aim is not to amend or implement the existing law of the state (such an aim would have been represented by a horizontal line from Quadrant C to B). Instead, it is first to exercise a natural law right—such as self-determination or the right to resist oppression—and then (if successful) to more radically revise or revitalize the domestic law of the state; thus the arrow first moves from Quadrant C to Quadrant D and only then perhaps to Quadrant B.

Because we are now largely in the realm of natural law (Quadrants C and D), it is useful to return to the general principles set out in the first half of this monograph—nondiscrimination, nonrepression, nonexploitation, and nonviolence—and ask, how can we say that a movement in question is manifesting a human rights "ethos" in its means and ends if it is not operating in relation to the positive law of human rights?

Maintenance of nonviolent discipline is an important indicator of commitment to human rights principles, but standing alone, it is not conclusive. Although most advocates of nonviolent resistance "suggest that it is a strategy particularly suited to advanc[ing] human rights and democracy" because of the complementarity of nonviolent means with the ends of peace, justice, freedom, and democracy, the "causes pursued through nonviolent action are not always virtuous."[233] Nonviolent resistance might lead to unintended negative consequences like the aftermath of the Arab Spring.[234] Due to the size and complexity of large-scale civil resistance movements, it is inevitable that many overlapping and perhaps even inconsistent aims may motivate participants. Indeed, motives may even shift and evolve over the course of a large-scale campaign. The efficacy of nonviolent resistance may also attract practitioners who want to "win" in the short term but who are not necessarily committed to democratic outcomes in the long-term. Finally, the negative goal of removing a repressive adversary that helped to mobilize and unify a large swath of the society against a regime may no longer be an effective glue to hold the movement together once the main target is gone. Disagreements may emerge about the movement's purposes and goals.

Despite the apparent difficulties in assessing whether a nonviolent movement is genuinely committed to human rights, this monograph takes important strides in defining criteria to do just that by identifying and analyzing specific types of evidence that civil resistance movements may generate and leave behind. The resulting typology, though preliminary, may allow an outside observer to begin to assess a movement's commitment to human rights standards before, during and after a campaign.

Evidence of Human Rights General Principles: Toward a Typology

A wide variety of evidence may be relevant to determining whether a civil resistance movement respects the general principles of human rights, including publicly articulated motives for coming together and resisting oppression; philosophical reflections and statements by movement leaders; movement signs (placards, banners), slogans, songs and poetry; movement education; and opinion polling that asks participants about their perception of the movement. All these different types of evidence may shed light on whether a particular movement is evincing a human rights *ethos*. What follows sets out some preliminary categories that may make up an eventual typology of evidence to be used in assessing whether and to what extent a civil resistance movement is manifesting such an *ethos*. Determining whether a civil resistance movement manifests such an *ethos* is important in determining whether a movement should be taken into account as we develop an analytical framework incorporating people power into international human rights law.

Statements by Movement Participants and Leaders

Movements can manifest human rights principles through formal or written statements by participants or leaders, such as manifestos or declarations. In some cases, especially the civil resistance struggles in the former Soviet bloc, there was an extensive and sophisticated philosophical reflection that preceded and to an extent accompanied the mass movements. Popular support for such statements and reflections is evidenced in the leadership role the figures authorizing these reflections played in mass civil resistance movements and in the popular elections afterwards. Some like Vaclav Havel were propelled to political power.

Havel wrote deep meditations like *The Power of the Powerless* that were circulated, along with his plays, in the underground *samizdat* literature that passed, unofficially and hand-to-hand, throughout the states of the former Soviet Union. These meditations clearly marked the centrality of human rights to his thought and cause. Havel analyzed the political conditions of the post-totalitarian system as one dominated by lies and various forms of official hypocrisy, a system where:

government by bureaucracy is called popular government; the working class is enslaved in the name of the working class; the complete degradation of the individual is presented as his ultimate liberation; depriving people of information is called making it available; the use of power to manipulate is called the public control of power, and the arbitrary abuse of power is called observing the legal code; the repression of culture is called its development; the expansion of imperial influence is presented as support for the oppressed; the lack of free expression becomes the highest form of freedom; farcical elections become the highest form of democracy; banning independent thought becomes the most scientific of world views; military occupation becomes fraternal assistance. Because the regime is captive to its own lies, it must falsify everything. It falsifies the past. It falsifies the present, and it falsifies the future. It falsifies statistics. It pretends not to possess an omnipotent and unprincipled police apparatus. It pretends to respect human rights. It pretends to persecute no one. It pretends to fear nothing. It pretends to pretend nothing.[235]

As a progenitor and signatory of Charter 77, a document produced by the Czechoslovak Helsinki watch group, Havel was committed to a strategy of invoking human rights against the government. However, he recognized that the first place where confrontation against the totalitarian system would play out, would not be "on the level of real, institutionalized, quantifiable power" but rather on the level of "human consciousness and conscience, the existential level," where a fundamental longing for human rights quietly burns.[236] Nevertheless, this existential power, he said, represents a "fifth column of social consciousness," it resides "in the hidden aims of life, in human beings repressed longing for dignity and fundamental rights, for the realization of their real social and political interests."[237] Aware that his status as "dissident" was at risk of setting him apart from "normal" Czechs and Slovaks, Havel reminded his readers that the "'dissident' movement grows out of the principle of equality, founded on the notion that human rights and freedoms are indivisible," and pointed out that "dissidents" had united to defend "unknown workers" and "unknown musicians."[238]

At the time Havel published *The Power of the Powerless*, revolution seemed a far-off dream. The "static and stable" conditions of the post-totalitarian state, Havel believed, were the precise opposite of the conditions necessary to incite revolt (either armed or unarmed). In view of this, the dissident strategy was a "legalistic" one, a "persistent and never-ending appeal to the laws," including international human rights. This might have seemed a futile and illusory form of resistance, given how Havel described the role of law in the post-totalitarian state: "If the exercise of power circulates through the whole power structure as blood flows through veins, then the legal code can be understood as something that reinforces the walls of those veins."[239] But Havel argued that the system "desperately" depended on the law—on a "noble" version of the law that support[ed] the system's lies—and was "hopelessly tied down by the necessity of pretending the laws are observed." Thus, it could not ignore legalistic appeals. The initial strategy of the Czechoslovak dissident movement involved invoking positive law—defending the human and civil rights "entrenched in various official documents such as the UDHR, the International Covenants on Human Rights, the Concluding Act of the Helsinki Agreement, and the constitutions of individual states."[240] Chartists committed themselves to defending anyone prosecuted for "acting in the spirit of those rights" and to acting "in the same spirit in their work," by pressuring the regime to defend those rights and calling attention to their lack.[241] "Demanding that the laws be upheld is thus an act of living within the truth that threatens the whole mendacious structure at its point of maximum mendacity."[242]

Though Havel was pessimistic about the realistic chances for revolt, it was only a decade later that a large-scale nonviolent movement broke out in Czechoslovakia, with Havel quickly emerging as its leader. During the Velvet Revolution, there were popular calls for him to assume political leadership of the country. Signs and even graffiti with the slogan "Havel na Hrad" appeared throughout the crowds gathered in Wenceslas Square.

Source: Elizabeth A. Wilson ©

This slogan can be translated as "Havel to the Castle," the castle (Pražský hrad) being the building that houses the government of then-Czechoslovakia, equivalent to the capitol or the White House. Havel was eventually elected president in the first free elections that took place in former Czechoslovakia in June 1990. Support for Havel was, at least to some extent, support for his human rights platform.

Movement Education

Consciousness-raising or consciousness-changing frequently accompanies nonviolent movements, often as part of creating institutions parallel to the "official" institutions that are being rejected by a nonviolent movement. Though Gandhi is most known for the successes of his civil disobedience campaigns—Gandhi on the beach at Dandi, gathering salt in the open defiance of British laws and "shaking the foundations of the British empire,"[243] is an indelible image of the power of the people to resist oppression—he himself considered more important his "constructive program" to reform Indian village life and prepare all strata of Indian society for independence. His constructive program included social reforms such as *khadi* (the making and wearing of domestic cloth) to lift India out of its trade dependence on Great Britain, the promotion of Hindu-Muslim unity, removal of untouchability, education in sanitation and hygiene, uplift of women, and basic and adult education, among other things.

The *samizdat* publications referred to above, the underground press and the culture of reading forbidden literature in Central and Eastern Europe under communism, all these were specific activities that were part of a constructive resistance program aiming to educate, raise awareness and awaken the mind of the people in spite of censorship, propaganda, and state repression. In *The Power of the Powerless*, Havel reflects on a hypothetical green grocer who places a sign in his window, amidst the onions and peppers—"Workers of the world, unite!"—a Marxist slogan, delivered from the state headquarters of his business along with the day's shipments of vegetables. What is the sign really saying, Havel asks? Is the green grocer really expressing his honest opinion that workers of the world should unite? Is he so enthusiastic about the idea that he cannot restrain himself from communicating it to the world? Or does his decision to put the sign in the window embody a different, subliminal message, one that says, "I, the greengrocer XY, live here and I know what I must do. I behave in the manner expected of me. I can be depended upon and am beyond reproach. I am obedient and therefore I have the right to be left in peace."[244] Havel thus shows that this small gesture is part of the fabric of "living a lie" that is required to survive in a political system build on lies. In such a "through the looking glass" world, electing to "live in truth" is to unleash a political power that is "singular, explosive, incalculable."[245] Should the green grocer one day decide not to display the sign, to stop voting in fake elections, to say what he really thinks at political meetings, he will be punished, but "[b]y breaking the rules of the game, he has disrupted the game as such... He has shattered the world of appearances, the fundamental pillar of the system."[246] Havel's meditation brings the reader to the self-conscious insight that lies behind nonviolent resistance—namely, that all power is ultimately dependent on the cooperation of those who are subject to it and that when this cooperation is withdrawn,

Gandhi at Dandi, South Gujarat, picking up salt on the beach at the end of the Salt March, April 1930. Source: Wikimedia Commons.

power in the long-run cannot survive.

Movement education may reflect human rights general principles by trying to foster awareness of the dignity of being human. One such effort was the "Black Consciousness Movement" (BCM) initiated by Steve Biko, during the anti-Apartheid struggle in South Africa. Although some have linked the BCM to the Soweto uprising and its violent aftermath, Biko himself embraced nonviolent resistance, perhaps for strategic more than moral reasons. In contrast to the underground and banned violent movement led in the mid-1970s by the African National Congress (ANC), which only in the 1980s moved away from armed insurrection, the BCM was committed to "overground" operation within the law, which strategically gave it more visibility to other South Africans, and thus, it massively increased the participation rate in nonviolent actions, such as boycotts, strikes or public demonstrations.

The premise of BCM was that colonialism has both objective and subjective aspects, and that before blacks could achieve outward liberation, they needed to free themselves inwardly. The South African Students' Organization (SASO) declared in a "Policy Manifesto":

> 4. a. SASO upholds the concept of black consciousness and the drive towards black awareness as the most logical and significant means of ridding ourselves of the shackles that bind us to perpetual servitude.
> b. SASO defines black consciousness as follows: Black consciousness is an attitude of mind, a way of life.
> i. The basic tenet of black consciousness is that the black man must reject all value systems that seek to make him a foreigner in the country of his birth and reduce his basic human dignity (italics added).[247]

BCM stressed that both sides in the Apartheid system needed to recognize their basic humanity, albeit in different ways:

> The most potent weapon of the oppressor is the mind of the oppressed. So as a prelude whites must be made to realise that they are only human, not superior. Same with Blacks. They must be made to realise that they are also human, not inferior.

Biko's insight was that "inhumanity" can work in two directions; the oppressed can feel less than human, while the oppressors can feel more than human: recognizing common "humanness" is a precondition for liberation on both sides. While the BCM counseled that blacks needed to exclude whites, in order to have space to develop a new consciousness, and so was exclusionary in the short term, the movement ultimately envisioned an integrated South Africa and felt that when consciousness was changed, this integration would happen naturally, driven by the force of equality, justice and fairness for all. Since the exclusionary aspect of BCM was a temporary strategy and was paired with principled nonviolent action, BCM arguably reflected a human rights *ethos*.

Another nonviolent resistance movement emerging from the black African population of South Africa also exemplifies some of the self-reliance advocated by SASO. Organized around the assertion of social and economic rights and rejecting dismissive treatment by the post-Apartheid government, the *Abahlali baseMjondolo* ("Residents of the Shacks" in Zulu) movement arose in the early 21st century when a community in the Durban slums spontaneously organized to block construction of a factory near their residences. Since then, the slum residents have organized to improve their conditions through constructive programs while resisting government efforts to clear the slums and eradicate their places of dwelling. *Abahlali* women have sowed community gardens and created cooperatives in order to improve quality of life.[248] *Abahlali* members engage shack dwellers in direct democracy and make leaders accountable to local committees. Dialogue is fostered through community meetings where people share stories of suffering and propose and debate solutions. These activities reject exploitation, manifest nonviolent discipline to a large extent, and foster social and political nondiscrimination within the community.

Public Opinion Survey Research

Evidence that a movement manifests a human rights *ethos* may be found through the more direct means of public opinion survey research or polling. Participants in a nonviolent movement may simply be asked about their motives, beliefs, feelings, objectives, or other relevant subjective states. While it may be impractical to conduct such polling in the middle of an active movement, it is not impossible, and researchers are beginning to do it.

Such a survey was done during the predominantly nonviolent Euromaidan revolution in 2013–2014.[249] Researchers stationed themselves near various entrances to protest sites and randomly stopped protesters to ask them to respond to survey questions and to answer short interview questions. Although the study was not focused on human rights *per se* but rather on the more limited question of the effect of social media on participation, the survey included a number of questions asking participants to describe the reasons why they were participating. Part of the research was designed to test a hypothesis put forward by the mobilization frames theorists Snow and Benford that "[p]eople are more likely to protest if the protest grievance is framed in a unifying rights discourse."[250]

The survey results from the Euromaidan revolution indicated that 33 percent of those polled were protesting because the government had infringed their rights. Although this was not as high a percentage as those who said they were protesting to secure a better future for Ukraine, researchers noted that protesters seemed to use the phrases, "I want a better future," "I have a right to a better future," and "My civil rights were violated" almost interchangeably.[251] Activists stated that the protests grew in size because they were successful in framing demands as rights, with one more radical activist stating that they tried to avoid "potentially divisive topics of state language" or other ethnolinguistic claims, explaining that these "would not win over the masses in Kyiv, not in 2014."[252] Online messages and posts evinced "dominance of citizenship, political rights, and anti-state discourse… as opposed to anti-Russophone, anti-Donbas discourse, which was more present in 2004 during the nonviolent Orange Revolution."[253] This research at Euromaidan uncovered that demands shifted in the direction of rights in response to the government's use of violence. At the outset of demonstrations, the central demands of protesters, as reflected in posters, slogans, and speeches, were "focused on socioeconomic and political development and the desire for the Europeanization of Ukraine."[254] Just as it seemed that the protests would not amount to a large mobilization, a group of students and journalists were brutally beaten by police on November 30, 2013. After that display of violence by the state, "demands shifted to a focus on the protection of universal human and civil rights." Shortly thereafter, turnout increased three- or fourfold to include an estimated 800,000 ordinary Ukrainians who joined the protest in later weeks,[255] more evidence that rights rhetoric—and the trampling of rights by the state and ensuing outrage—promoted participation.

The Euromaidan survey is fairly unusual, especially for its timely "on the ground" methodology and analytical sophistication. Although not designed to glean whether the movement reflected a human rights *ethos* generally, the study showed a sophisticated grasp of human rights in constructing survey questions and analyzing the answers given by movement participants.

Another survey carried out shortly after the Tunisian and Egyptian revolutions in 2011 does not show as sophisticated an understanding of human rights discourse as the Euromaidan analysis. The "Arab Barometer" survey provides some insight into the Tunisian and Egyptian revolutions, but it also shows that unless survey questions about human rights are drawn up with care, the survey results will be less than illuminating.[256] Survey respondents were given nine choices (and "other") for why they participated in the demonstrations, none of which was framed in terms of rights. The closest to a human rights option was "1. Civil and political freedoms, and emancipation from oppression." Three other choices were difficult to distinguish: "2. Betterment of the economic situation; 6. Increased social justice; and 9. Social and economic justice."[257] The results of the survey led researchers to conclude that "participants in both revolutions believed overwhelmingly that they were about economic concerns, and only minorities of participants believed that they were primarily about civil and political liberties." This analysis reflects a narrow view of rights as being only about civil and political freedoms, not social and economic rights, and it does not unpack the notion of "justice" as implicating rights. The sentiment in a slogan like "jobs are a basic human right, you corruption mafia," popular during the Jasmine Revolution in Tunisia, would not be easily captured by the set of questions used in the Arab Barometer survey. Unless questions are framed with an awareness of human rights principles in mind, research results might be misleading.

Still, if designed with a sophisticated understanding of human rights as including the general principle of nonexploitation (focused on socioeconomic rights), such surveys can be an authoritative source to help determine how participants in nonviolent movements understand their demands. It is not necessary that participants subjectively understand their actions to be aimed at realizing "human rights" as such in order to determine whether a movement reflects a human rights *ethos*, because it is possible for a movement to manifest human rights principles without utilizing the vocabulary of "human rights." Grassroots protesters may more likely refer to "rights," rather than "human rights," or even simply "demands," and these references would then have to be contextualized into the other evidence described below from the movement to determine the presence of a human rights *ethos*. To the extent that subjective understandings reflect one of the principles of nondiscrimination, nonrepression, nonexploitation and nonviolence without negating any of the others, they suggest that participants are embracing a human rights *ethos*.

Signs, Slogans, Songs and Poetry

Signs, slogans, poetry, songs and other ephemera that people power movements produce specifically invoking human rights, principles or associated ends—freedom, justice, peace—may provide *prima facie* evidence that participants were motivated to realize human rights through their struggle.[258] Such evidence may be transitory, intended to influence the day-to-day evolution and development of a movement, without thought of posterity. But precisely for that reason, it may provide valuable insight into the inner workings of a movement. The

Bahrain, 2011. Source: Flickr user Al Jazeera English, via Creative Commons.

widespread use of cell phones and video and dissemination through social media make it more possible than ever before to preserve the ephemera of civil resistance movements. Perhaps requiring interpretation, these expressive signs, symbols, and signifiers may be indirect and imperfect indicators of the motives for people participating in civil resistance movements, but until systematic empirical studies (either qualitative or quantitative) are able to be carried out, they can provide a rough proxy for the opinions and beliefs motivating civil resisters, especially if they are widely circulated and repeated. At the same time, broad appeal of such expressive signifiers might even have advantages over interviews, since not all individuals motivated to participate in a civil resistance movement may be equally able to articulate their motivations in language. The creative outputs of individuals who are expressively gifted may give voice to others. Expressive signs and signifiers may give voice to unconscious or unacknowledged motives. Assessing such evidence will be more of an art than a science.[259]

In revolutionary movements, slogans may not generally speak to specific human rights but to more abstract and general expressions of popular sovereignty. According to Sidiki, during the Arab Spring, "No other phrase spread as fast and as wide as '*al'sha'b yureed*' ('the people's will')—it was contagious across countries, being heard also in Cairo, Sanaa, and Damascus."[260] Though not expressing a specific right protected in any treaty, "the people's will" speaks to a demand that government be based on the will of the people and be responsive to the people's demands—a clearly understandable demand for popular sovereignty and freedom from repression.[261] Other ways of expressing a similar sentiment are slogans reflecting imperatives to "leave," "resign," or "dégage," which could be seen as efforts to reclaim sovereignty from the "official" government. In Tunisia statements of national liberation were often paired with *thawrat al-hurriyyah wa al* (freedom and rights, no president forever), indicating a desire to be free of indefinite autocratic rule and thus reflecting the nonrepression principle.[262]

Songs and music may have more or less immediate impacts on nonviolent movements, or alternatively may be aimed at longer term transformations of consciousness. The South African musician and musicologist Johnny Clegg violated Apartheid laws by collaborating with Zulu musician Sipho Mchunu to form the interracial band Juluka, enacting in his life and music the principle of nondiscrimination. At the time, in the early 1970s, media in South Africa was tightly controlled by the government—television was not even permitted in the country until 1976—and Juluka could not be played on government-controlled radio. But in 1979, an independent radio station, Capital Radio 604, was started in the "independent" Bantustan Transkei that gave considerable airplay to Juluka and generally supported the anti-Apartheid movement by broadcasting "unofficial" real news to South Africa and the world.

As in the BCM, consciousness raising and consciousness changing was Clegg's ultimate objective, though not necessarily tied to one or another specific protest. In the song, "Scatterlings [nomads, wanderers] of Africa," the narrator first sees the "scatterlings" as separate from himself, referring to them as "they" and singing of his love for "each uprooted one." But the humanity of the scatterlings is evident, amid the "broken wall / bicycle wheel" where the "magic machine cannot match / human being human being." By the end of the song, the narrator discovers that "[m]y very first beginnings... Lie deeply buried / In the dust of Olduvai"—a gorge in Africa where the bones of Lucy, our first ancestor, were discovered. He realizes then that he too is a scatterling of Africa.

> And we are scatterlings of Africa /
> Both you and I /
> We are on the road to Phelamanga /
> Beneath a copper sky /

"Phelamanga" is said to be a mythical, invented place, usually translated as "the place where lies end," presumably the lies of Apartheid.

Writing songs in both Zulu and English and performing with traditional Zulu dancers, Clegg deeply immersed himself in Zulu culture, earning the epithet of "the White Zulu," or *Le Zulu Blanc*. In an age where race-crossings are reflexively viewed as politically incorrect, what Clegg did might be condemned today as "culturally appropriating" the Zulu experience, but clearly that is not how his Zulu brothers saw it. He committed to suffer with those oppressed by Apartheid and to use music to break barriers. Juluka disbanded in 1986, under considerable pressure and threats from the South African government, but not before crafting stunning fusions of Western and Zulu music, and Clegg later went on to form another interracial band, Savuka. In a political context forbidding the mixing of races, the artistic decision to fuse musical traditions was transgressive and radical while furthering human rights, particularly those of equality and nondiscrimination.

Legal and Institutional Outcomes

Recognition of human rights in the institutional outcomes resulting from nonviolent uprisings is the best and most probative indicator of whether a movement can be characterized as having a human rights *ethos*. Perhaps the clearest outcome is the adoption of a new constitution protecting human rights. Depending on the array of rights protected, human rights provisions can reflect some or all of the general principles of human rights, as well as democratic goals and aspiration for peaceful change.

A human rights-respecting constitution was adopted in South Africa after the victory of the nonviolent resistance led by the United Democratic Front (UDF), supported by the ANC. Legal scholar Mutua has described the construction of the post-Apartheid state in South Africa as "the first deliberate and calculated effort in history to craft a human rights state—a policy that is primarily based on human rights norms."[263] Relevant to the monograph's argument that constitutional rights provisions may reflect, or sediment, the work of civil resistance movements, the South African constitution has been said to "represent[ ] the vindication of decades of human rights activism."[264] The first article of the South African constitution declares the following:

> The Republic of South Africa is one, sovereign, democratic state founded on the following values:

a) Human dignity, the achievement of equality and the advancement of human rights and freedoms.

b) Non-racialism and non-sexism.

The South African constitution protects various other human rights. Its recognition of social and economic rights is particularly significant, in light of criticism that the South African transition focused narrowly on civil and political rights and did little to affect the underlying economic disparities created by the Apartheid system. The presence in the constitution of guarantees of social and economic rights gives a constitutional foothold for legal challenges aimed at vindicating such rights.

Post-revolutionary constitutions respecting human rights were also adopted in Tunisia and Poland.[265] Czechoslovakia adopted a Constitution Act in 1991 incorporating the Charter of Fundamental Rights and Freedoms, although the constitutional status of the Charter is ambiguous in the aftermath of the split-up of the federation into the Czech Republic and Slovakia.[266] (The status of the Charter is not ambiguous in Slovakia, where it has been incorporated into the constitution.) The former East Germany acceded to the West German constitution, with its human rights protections, after "die Wende" in 1989. Two countries—Serbia and Georgia —that saw peaceful revolutions against authoritarian regimes in 2000 and 2003, respectively, adopted constitutions that protect human rights directly.

Mixed Motives and Trojan Horses: Ambiguous or Countervailing Evidence

Large-scale mass mobilizations may be driven by a mix of motives, and the particular balance of motives may vary from movement to movement. In assessing civil resistance movements and the presence or absence of a human rights *ethos*, researchers may encounter ambiguous or countervailing evidence. This final subsection considers some examples of such evidence and contexts in which they may appear.

Expressions of Patriotism

One example of an ambiguous piece of evidence is the expression of patriotism There is no necessary contradiction between slogans seeking liberation of the nation, or even glorifying the nation, and those expressing human rights ideals. Mere expressions of patriotic love of country have to be distinguished from more exclusionary nationalist sentiments. Demonstrators in Maidan Square in 2013–2014 appealed to patriotic feelings, often breaking out into impromptu renditions of the Ukrainian national anthem. Poetry recited to demonstrators invoked the beauty of the land. Chants proclaimed, "Glory to Ukraine! Glory to the heroes." The lyrics to a song exhorted, "Rise up my country, rise up my people."[267] An often-graffitied phrase in Tunisia was *Tunis hurra* (Tunisia is free), but there was a notable absence of slogans proclaiming "Tunisia is great!"[268] During Euromaidan, a speaker encouraged protesters: "Have courage to become normal people. And I will die with you. And Ukraine will live happily with other nations," words that indicate an absence of xenophobia.[269] A movement consisting of a diverse collective of people seeking to fundamentally reimagine (not abolish) the state in which they find themselves can be as reflective of human rights norms as formal legal complaints to international treaty bodies, if not more so.

However, if expressions of patriotism are interwoven with violent ideology, or are combined with hate speech or discriminatory acts against particular minority groups, this could be evidence that the movement is no longer organized to reflect a human rights *ethos*. If expressed by a violent flank or by individuals who engage in threats or acts of violence, such as sexual assaults on women as occurred during the post-Tahrir protests in Egypt between 2012–2013 (some surely perpetrated by the state agents posing as activists), patriotic sentiments would have to be read as not reflecting a human rights *ethos*. although it should be noted, as reflected in the Joint Report of the special rapporteurs discussed in Chapter III, that isolated acts of violence are in themselves not enough to transform a nonviolent movement into a violent one.

When a violent flank accompanies a nonviolent movement, relevant information to assessing the human rights *bona fides* of the movement would be how large is the violent flank compared to the nonviolent movement; how clearly the violent flank can be distinguished from the nonviolent movement; whether the violent flank exists as part of the movement or outside of it, even if it espouses the same objectives, and how acts or threats of violence are responded to by the nonviolent movement.[270] Well-organized movements can prepare for violent flanks or agents provocateurs infiltrating demonstrations through various means, e.g., holding sessions in advance to warn of infiltrators or those not committed to human rights aims; assigning "wardens" or movement marshals with armbands to help maintain discipline; asking participants to wear a certain color to identify themselves; physically isolating violent individuals during ongoing protests, ejecting them from the demonstrations, or even handing them over to the police; and utilizing amplifiers and other means to convey the purposes of the campaign.

Insults and Threats of Violence

Insults and threats of violence are other types of countervailing evidence. Of course, expressions of negative or hostile emotions, even death threats or wishes, may represent mere venting of emotion and not automatically disqualify a movement from being recognized as a human rights movement. It is not unheard of for some elements in a nonviolent movement to suggest that if the nonviolent protest does not succeed, violence may ensue. However, since nonviolent resistance is a means of waging conflict "without the threat or use of violence," theoreticians of nonviolent resistance place a high premium on the importance of maintaining nonviolent discipline. A nonviolent movement that holds violence as a trump card creates an atmosphere of latent violence that may inhibit the movement's success. It may be satisfying for the participants in revolutionary movements to "turn the tables" and bring low the high and mighty through insults and degradation, but in order to maintain nonviolent discipline, it seems advisable for organizers to try to limit expressions that might be taken as, or really be, incitements to hatred, discrimination, or violence.

This image (on the opposite page) of Arab dictators, hand-cuffed, dressed in orange prison jumpsuits, with nooses around their necks, shows so much creativity and artistic merit that it seems a sublimation of violent impulses, satisfying them through fantasy rather than incitement to actual violence. It also implies that some kind of legal process has been undergone and the dictators have been judged: guilty. In the case of South Africa, nonviolent protesters, dressed in military-like uniforms, carried wooden or cartoon-made weapons, not to idolize violent struggle but to symbolize popular resistance in general and perhaps also make the point that nonviolent struggle is not pacifism but war by other means. One researcher and a former ANC member coined the term "iconography of violence" to describe such representations present in nonviolent demonstrations.[271]

Finally, to the extent it can be discerned, context is important. The same (type of) image could function differently in different contexts. For example, Libya did not have a disciplined and sustained nonviolent movement, so such an image might function to encourage violence in the Libyan context, whereas it might not so function in the context of the more disciplined Tunisian movement.

Source: "Symbols and Slogans of the Arab Spring," Qantara, https://en.qantara.de/content/symbols-and-slogans-arab-spring?page=3.

Assessing the commitment to human rights of a nonviolent movement may also be of interest to participants. The efficacy of nonviolent movements may attract some participants who are not sincerely committed to human rights or democracy, or to power-sharing with coalitions that want to promote human rights and democracy. Nonviolent revolutions may contain "Trojan horses," elements that join in nonviolent movements in order to seize power with the aims of ultimately eliminating, rather than sharing power with, political opponents, or of instituting non-democratic regimes.

Egypt and Iran present examples of nonviolent revolutions that succeeded only in the short-term or did not succeed at all because the nonviolent coalitions in these countries either contained "Trojan horses" or brought to power third parties that were not committed to democracy (e.g., the military or the Islamists)[272]. For example, opposition to the Western-backed Shah in Iran came from two main constituencies—the middle-class and liberal intelligentsia on the one hand and the Islamists on the other.[273] The grand Ayatollah Ruhollah Khomeini was exiled from the country in 1964, after which he began to conceive the idea of an Islamic Republic. The revolution succeeded only when nonviolent resistance gained the upper hand, eventually widening in support to include many segments of society, students, teachers, and especially workers.[274] Although liberals and Islamists worked together to depose the Shah, Khomeini was not committed to working with liberals in the long term. Within a few months, liberals were forced out of the post-revolutionary cabinet, and eventually close to 20,000 people were killed as Khomeini consolidated power.[275] Chenoweth and Stephan conclude: "Exiled leadership played a large role in the uprising, which revolved around Khomeini's charisma rather than a durable commitment from different parts of the opposition to build a democratic state after the Shah."[276]

While Iran's negative outcome of an authoritarian government coming to power following a mass nonviolent campaign simply may have been anomalous,[277] it appears that groups that were allies in resistance during the movement did not want to look too closely at the long-term prospects for cooperation in governance. Khomeini was not completely explicit about his ideas for governance in the post-revolutionary Iran (which were anything but compatible with democratic pluralism), and the liberal opposition may have preferred to remain ignorant of this long-term incompatibility rather than abort the revolution.[278]

The Egyptian case was slightly different, though it also involved a civil resistance movement where Islamists and secular liberals joined forces to depose an autocratic and unpopular ruler, Hosni Mubarak. A feature of the Egyptian revolution was that the military, largely as a whole, withdrew its "pillar of support" from Mubarak and sided with the people, winning hearts and minds in the process. In the first round of parliamentary elections held after the revolution in 2011, the Muslim Brotherhood was better organized institutionally than other groups that had participated in the movement deposing Mubarak. The Brotherhood thus came to power without the need for, but also without the internal culture to work with, and govern in, a coalition with other partners, particularly liberal and secular groups.[279] Mohamed Morsi, Muslim Brotherhood member and the elected president in 2012, then undertook to rule in a way that alienated other groups and led some Egyptians to believe that he was fashioning himself into a dictator and transforming Egypt into an Islamist state.[280] A second wave of mass protests were organized in 2013, but this time the revolutionaries did not deploy their power as they had in the first revolution. Rather, they closely colluded with the military, asking it to intervene, depose the ruler and take over the government. Perhaps because the decision to withdraw support in the first revolution was made at high levels of the military and was not a matter of individual soldiers abandoning their roles, the military remained an intact force. The second Egyptian revolution therefore cannot strictly speaking be called peaceful (and thus identified as having a human rights *ethos)* because it was effected through the implied violent force of the Egyptian military; it was a military coup that rode to power on the back of popular mobilization.[281]

Although it may be difficult to avoid entirely Trojan horses, activists may want to keep in mind the possibility that they exist and perhaps make a greater determination to engage in constructive resistance programs, building resilient institutions, instilling human rights' practices, and developing monitoring and accountability tools, in order to be better prepared should they actually be successful in their campaigns and need to take power. Assessing the human rights *ethos* of a movement may thus be relevant for movement participants, and the typology outlined here may aid in helping them make the correct assessment.

To conclude this discussion regarding evidence, what we have been doing here is creating methodological criteria for assessing when a large-scale civil resistance campaign aimed at realizing ends not recognized in human rights positive law may be understood nonetheless as imbued with a human rights *ethos*. Once these criteria are established and applied, it means that we can take the practice of particular campaigns into account as we look for evidence of general principles across international and domestic, positive and natural law. In this way, civil resistance movements can become cognizable in international law beyond being a means of implementing positive law. Not all evidence should be given equal weight of course—a constitution enacted on the heels of nonviolent victory obviously outweighs an isolated slogan graffitied across a wall—but the precise weight given to any particular piece of evidence is likely to vary from campaign to campaign, depending in part on the particular tactics adopted by the movement in question. This leads to the next and final step in this analysis—namely, understanding how people power movements can be understood as a source of positive international law.

Chapter VI
Making International Law Human Rights Law

*I*n this final part, the monograph returns the analysis to positive law by theorizing how people power movements can be understood as making positive international law. While most people power movements register their effects on domestic law, this last part of the monograph argues that people power movements also impact international law. Since in every practical sense people power creates and maintains states, it is a fiction to assign sovereign power only to states as international law traditionally does. The following offers three theories, in relation to three different substantive areas of international law, through which people power can be seen as not just shaping international law but actually making it.

The movement between dimensions that we are concerned with here can be visualized (see Box 7) as an arrow representing movement that would flow from Quadrant D back to Quadrant A, as the effects of people power movements are potentially registered in the positive law of international human rights. This could happen through the inchoate or incipient formation of customary international law, or through alternative yet-to-be theorized means. The fourth scenario here is hypothetical because it represents the argument being presently made in this monograph. It is not settled or even developing law. Consequently, it is represented with a dotted line. This arrow is conceptual, rather than sociological—it does not represent a change in anything happening on the ground. Rather, it represents a change in how legal scholars and jurists can interpret what is happening on the ground as they determine international law and say what the law is.

Box 7. Visualization of effects of people power movements registered in the positive law of international human rights

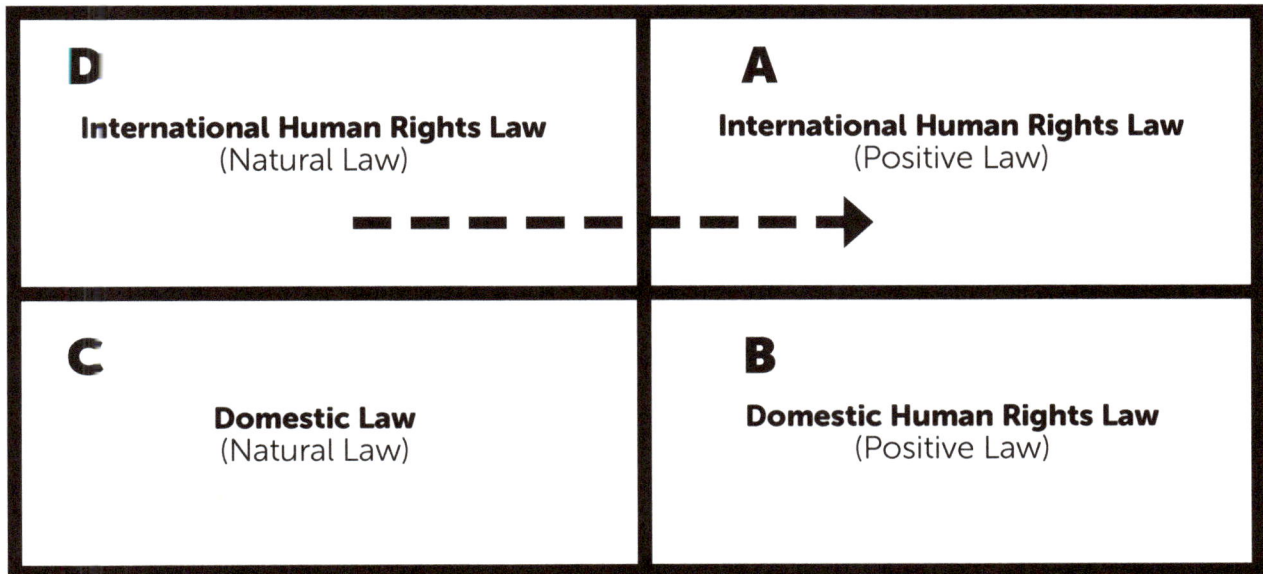

D **International Human Rights Law** (Natural Law)	**A** **International Human Rights Law** (Positive Law)
C **Domestic Law** (Natural Law)	**B** **Domestic Human Rights Law** (Positive Law)

The monograph presents these theories in order of how radically they depart from existing understandings of how international law works.

First, where customary law is still developing and where state practice alone might be inconclusive, a widespread pattern or practice of nonviolent movements might supply evidence of *opinio juris* supporting the emergence of a customary international norm. The first section below looks at how people power could function in this way. Prosecution for human rights abuses is largely a matter of customary law; outside of the Convention Against Torture, the Genocide Convention, and the Geneva Conventions, no treaties require that perpetrators of human rights violations be prosecuted. But state practice induced by people power movements reflecting general principles of human rights may supply a sense of *opinio juris* that the state action, considered alone, may not have.

Second, in a situation where international human rights law does not recognize a particular right, a contrary understanding held by participants of nonviolent civil resistance movements arguably should take precedence, especially when there is a widespread and consistent pattern of behaviors and actions on the part of movement participants that reflect this understanding. In this situation, people power would be evidence of a right reflecting the general principles of human rights. In the case of corruption, for example, there is dissonance between the international legal community's view and the more grassroots view that is driving the proliferation of people-powered anti-corruption activities worldwide. International human rights law does not recognize a right to be free from corruption as a human right, characterizing it instead as a criminal matter. But activists often do see it as a human right.

Third and most radically, it can be argued that people power movements, if mobilized on a sufficiently large-scale, are a different sort of *sui generis* source of law, one that is realizing the natural right of political self-determination. The third section below argues that when nonviolent civil resistance movements respecting human rights general principles reach a certain scale and intensity, they are activating a "dormant social contract" and reclaiming sovereignty and thus taking law-making power back from the state. This arguably activates a right to democracy under particular conditions for a particular people in a particular state context, irrespective of whether a right to democracy has coalesced as a right under general customary international law.

Prosecutions and Transitional Justice

"Transitional justice" is the term that has been coined to describe mechanisms used to achieve accountability for human rights violations after a societal transition to peace or democracy. These mechanisms may include criminal tribunals; truth commissions; lustrations and restitution; or community reconciliation. This subsection focusses on criminal accountability as part of the transition process.

As originally conceived, the international human rights legal regime did not require criminal prosecutions for human rights violations, except in the narrow cases of torture and genocide. Article 14 of the ICCPR requires signatory states to compensate individuals whose rights under the treaty have been violated, but that article refers to a civil remedy and does not require prosecution of those responsible for the violation. Nevertheless, there has been steady progress toward a developing customary rule that prosecutions are required for serious human rights abuses, although this has not yet coalesced into a customary norm. The creation of the International Criminal Court (ICC)—now with 123 member states—indicates the growing acceptance that legal accountability must follow serious human rights violations.[282] Also important for transitional justice have been comestic or mixed domestic and international tribunals that have been created in states that have been transitioning to democracy, like South Africa, Argentina, and Chile, or recovering from mass atrocities, like Rwanda, or negotiating a peace after a civil war, like Sierra Leone.

Like human rights generally, the topic of transitional justice has been dominated by legal scholars who look at it through a legal lens. This legal focus means the role and impact of people power movements or campaigns in bringing about transitional justice mechanisms has been underestimated, or ignored. For example, many of the case studies Sikkink examined in her book *The Justice Cascade* focus on the role of lawyers and legal scholars and advocates or other elites and their institutional work in bringing about transitional justice mechanisms.[283] But a comparison with the cases included in the NAVCO database created by Chenoweth and Stephan shows that, in many cases, transitional justice mechanisms were created in response to extra-institutional nonviolent actions of civil resistance movements that occurred either concurrently with or shortly before in the studied countries.

Indeed, people power has already played a role in the modern movement toward accountability for human rights violations.[284] For example, the work of many CSO coalitions in Latin American countries that pressured newly-democratic states to set up transitional justice mechanisms and hold perpetrators of major human rights violations accountable for their crimes often occurred against a backdrop of large-scale civil resistance campaigns that called for prosecution of past human rights abuses. These campaigns, together with the work of CSOs, induced specific state practice and arguably reflected the view that justice in its natural law aspect required prosecutions. The calls for justice here were not based on positive law, as such positive law did not yet exist; they were calling for positive law to be brought into existence as a necessary element of the transition from dictatorship.

The Greek case is a good example of how research on transnational advocacy networks and traditional CSOs neglects the role of people power movements in bringing about transitional justice mechanisms.[285] In July 1974, large-scale nonviolent demonstrations led to the ouster of a military junta, an action that Chenoweth and Stephan classified as a successful nonviolent campaign. Public demands for accountability emerged as soon as a month after the transition. Newspapers from the time recorded "a growing public demand for retribution against the former dictators."[286] The first public calls for prosecutions were actually made, according to Sikkink, by a resistance organization called Democratic Defense, although no specific details are provided. By early September 1974, private criminal cases were beginning to be filed in Greek courts, initially for treason and mutiny, later for torture and murder.[287] In early October, the new government of Constantine Karamanlis signed a decree making it clear that an amnesty law passed after the fall of the junta to provide clemency to former political leaders did not apply to top leaders of the former regime.[288]

In her analysis, Sikkink focusses mainly on the somewhat tragic figure of Karamanlis and his personal desire to redeem his reputation from earlier association with the murder of an antifascist resistance icon and leftist Member of Parliament Gregoris Lambrakis. When Sikkink was conducting research for her book, the brother of then-deceased Karamanlis said that his brother "was obeying the feelings of the Greek people" in agreeing to trials.[289] Sikkink seems to find this an unsatisfying answer and does not pursue it further to establish a link between this opinion and a possible role and impact of the mobilized Greek citizenry on the streets of major cities.

Though not in great detail, legal scholar Roht-Arriaza examined the Greek case in considering the question of whether a customary law has formed requiring states to prosecute perpetrators of gross human rights violations. Without considering the people power demonstrations that led to the regime's fall, she concluded that it was difficult to ascertain whether the purges and prosecutions were occurring as a result of a sense of legal obligation (*opinio juris*) or because of "domestic political concerns."[290] But if "domestic political concerns" included the people's sense that natural justice required prosecutions, a people-powered *opinio juris* can be discerned.

Another example of successful transitional justice with a clear people power movement role is Argentina. While the first calls for prosecutions there came from the IACHR,[291] grassroots informal civic groups and established human rights organizations played an important role. The Mothers of the Disappeared (*Madres de la Plaza de Mayo*) and their resistance actions is one of the most well-known groups, but also active was the Grandmothers of the Disappeared. In addition, organizations such the Permanent Assembly for Human Rights, the Center for Legal and Social Studies, the Ecumenical Movement for Human Rights, and the Peace and Justice Service (SERPAJ) were also present and involved. When the IACHR arrived in Argentina for an in-country investigation, all these groups closely coordinated with investigators and arranged interviews with hundreds of victims and their families.[292] Ultimately, the IACHR published a searing critical report, calling on authorities to "initiate the corresponding investigations, to bring to trial and to punish, with the full force of the law, those responsible."[293] As the hold on power of the junta grew more tenuous—the result of the ongoing mobilization of ordinary Argentinians inspired by the protests and resilience of the Mothers of the Disappeared and other groups—demands for prosecutions became more pronounced, and by 1983, the year the military stepped down, the phrase "Trials and Punishment for All the Guilty" (*Juicio y Castigo a Todos los Culpables*) "became both a slogan and a primary demand of the human rights movement in Argentina."[294]

The move to actualizing this demand was made easier when a member of a human rights organization, Raul Alfonsin, was elected president in 1983. Alfonsin however initially hesitated to push for prosecutions. Before leaving power, the junta had adopted an amnesty law protecting everyone associated with the regime from prosecution, which was protested by more than 40,000 people marching in the streets of Buenos Aires. Despite the law, the Alfonsin government proceeded with prosecutions against top military leaders. When the trials threatened to expand from top leaders to large swathes of lower-level military officials (through private lawsuits initiated by victims or their families), the military attempted a coup; but the public demonstrated its support for the Alfonsin government through massive gatherings in front of the Congress building. The government survived, though felt it necessary to adopt an amnesty law blocking future trials, and a subsequent government pardoned the top leaders who had already been convicted. However, the will to prosecute survived, due in no small measure to the ongoing mobilization and persistence of civic groups such as the Mothers of the Disappeared demanding the right to justice and the right to know what had happened to their loved ones. The amnesty law was formally struck down by the Supreme Court in 2005 and repealed by Parliament. Court cases against military officials in Argentina slowly resumed.[295]

Takeaway

This monograph has set out parameters for ascertaining whether a particular civil resistance movement may be characterized as evincing a human rights *ethos*. We can go on to argue that state practice that is undertaken in response to the resolve of sustained and well-organized people power movements that demonstrate such an *ethos*—demanding prosecutions because rights have been violated and justice must be done—should not be seen as simply responding to "domestic political concerns." They are responding to such concerns, yes, but it is arguable that, when the parameters here are met, those domestic concerns embed a legal demand and reflect a sense of legal obligation with relevance to international law.

Thus, one way of incorporating "people power" into international law in a lawmaking capacity is to see it as supplying the *opinio juris* element necessary for the formation of customary international law—the sense that a certain act (or omission) is legally obligated. Evidence for people power as *opinio juris* may be easier to ascertain and more relevant in the case of human rights law than the "subjective" understanding of the state as to the motives behind its actions.

Right to be Free from Corruption

Government corruption is often a powerful impetus for people power movements. Rage at the greed and criminality of those in power may be as important as repression and physical integrity violations in provoking widespread civil resistance.

Rage at the corruption of the Ferdinand Marcos government in the Philippines in the 1980s was a major factor behind the People Power Revolution or the "Yellow Revolution" as it is sometimes called. The thousands of shoes belonging to Marcos's wife Imelda became a potent symbol of the corruption in that country. Anger with corruption has continued to simmer in Philippine politics, as neither the Aquino government that came to power after Marcos's ouster in 1986 nor subsequent governments have managed to bring corruption under control.[296] Beyerle notes, "[C]orruption is a grievance around which citizens mobilize in many nonviolent movements targeting authoritarian regimes. Examples can be found across the globe, from the People Power I and II revolutions in the Philippines, the nonviolent resistance to Serbian dictator, Slobodan Milosevic, led by the youth movement, OTPOR, the Rose Revolution in Georgia, to the nonviolent uprisings in Tunisia, Egypt and Yemen, and the two Orange Revolutions in Ukraine."[297] Elsewhere, others acknowledge: "It is notable how frequently corruption now unleashes protests, whether in authoritarian, semi-authoritarian, or democratic countries.... As has been extensively documented and analyzed by corruption specialists, public awareness of corruption and anger about it have grown massively in the world during the past twenty years."[298]

Despite the catalyzing effect of corruption on people power movements, the international community has approached anti-corruption as a matter of criminal law, rather than viewing the right to be free from corruption as a free-standing human right. If anti-corruption is thought of in relation to human rights at all, it is usually considered a means to the realization of rights.[299] Anti-corruption efforts in international law strive to regulate corruption through such treaties as the United Nations Convention Against Corruption (UNCAC) and the Organization for Economic Co-operation and Development Convention on Combatting Bribery of Foreign Public Officials in International Business Transactions. In a Forward to UNCAC, Kofi Annan described corruption "as an insidious plague" that "undermines democracy and the rule of law, leads to violations of human rights, distorts markets, erodes the quality of life and allows organized crime, terrorism and other threats to human security to flourish."[300] The US Foreign Corrupt Practices Act (FCPA) likewise treats corruption as a criminal offense.

The problem with a criminal law approach to corruption is that corruption is construed as an offense against the state, rather than the people who actually suffer from it. And as with all of international law, there is an enforcement problem. The UNCAC depends upon the state (filled with corrupt officials) to implement and enforce the convention. Domestic laws may also be limited. The powerful FCPA criminalizes only the paying of bribes, not solicitation, so foreign officials are not threatened with prosecution. Because of issues of foreign official immunity and reciprocity, state officials hesitate to prosecute other officials. But most corruption is not initiated by corporations, unless the corporation knows from prior experience that bribing officials is the way to get things done. Grand corruption results from culture and long-standing political and business relationships, while petty corruption permeates everyday life with distrust and back-dealing.

Despite intensive efforts to combat corruption through international and transnational cooperation, progress has been slow. In 2015, researchers Murray and Spalding concluded, "Both the political will and imperative to eliminate corruption remain weak. Though international and domestic legal regimes explicitly prohibit corruption, states have not generally enforced applicable laws effectively."[301] Supporting their claim, a 2016 survey found that more than 77% of 637 businesspeople polled in 19 Latin American countries believe their country's anti-corruption laws are ineffective. Over 50% believed that they had lost business because of corruption, but most declined to report corruption to the authorities. Of those who made reports to the government, 71% say the government failed to investigate.[302] State prosecutors often face high burdens of proof that make prosecution difficult. Murray and Spalding continued,

"Too many nations enable corrupt officials and provide the means to help hide the evidence. Leaders tacitly approve many forms of bribery in the name of national security, economic development or exigent circumstances."[303]

Source: "Moldova has just run out of cash," New Europe, https://neurope.eu/article/moldova-is-running-out-of-cash/.[304]

The Right to be Free from Corruption as a Human Right

In view of the slow progress made in combatting corruption through international efforts, Spalding has made a case that freedom from corruption should be independently recognized as a free-standing human right.[305] Such recognition could have three advantages, he argues. Firstly, it could add urgency to anti-corruption efforts, since rights that are seen as human rights are regarded as weightier and more urgent than other rights or legal claims. Secondly, it could undermine the most common justification for corruption—that "it is cultural." Since human rights are, by definition, "universal," seeing freedom from corruption as a human right strips away legitimacy from the argument that because they are "cultural," graft and bribes or corruption in general should be acceptable, laying bare the elements of "excuse" in this justification. Thirdly, and most importantly, seeing freedom from corruption as a human right would end the "perverse result."[306] The "perverse result" means that companies that do not wish to violate the law end up withdrawing from the country while so-called "black knights"—companies that feel free to engage with corrupt officials—move in to fill the void.[307] Hence, there is more corruption, not less. A human right to be free from corruption would arguably make the "black knights" more accountable, set up a stronger normative environment for more stringent corporate social responsibility and facilitate adoption of domestic anti-corruption legislations aiming to keep the work of domestic corporate business in other countries corruption free.

To make his case, Spalding argues from natural law, basing his argument on John Locke's theory of government, for two main reasons: first, the conduct involved in corruption is central to Locke's theory and second, because it is governments in the Anglo-Saxon world that have taken the greatest initiatives in combatting corruption worldwide. Locke's theory—so influential on the US and French revolutionaries—is that civil society is grounded on the consent of those who willingly give up the liberty they enjoy in the state of nature for the greater advantages of living under a [legislator] "bound to govern by established standing laws, promulgated and known by the people, and not by extemporary decrees." This government should have "no other end than the peace, safety, and public good of the people." Indeed, the very definition of legitimate political power is the "right of making laws... only for the public good."[308] The liberty of man in society is "to have a standing rule to live by, common to every one of that society, and made by the legislative power... not to be subject to the inconstant, uncertain, unknown, arbitrary will of another man."[309] Being subject to the arbitrary will of another, Spalding concludes, is the essence of corruption:

> Official conduct that procures a benefit in violation of official duty, and contrary to the rights of others, is but another way of describing the failure to govern by standing laws directed to the public good. Where the government has ceased to rule by standing laws without preference, where benefits are granted contrary to official duty and the rights of others, citizens "have no such decisive power to appeal to, [and] they are still in the state of Nature." Corruption thus voids the social contract, destroys government, and returns society to a state of nature. Indeed, when Locke defines tyranny as "making use of the power any one has in his hands not for the good of those who are under it, but for his own private, separate advantage," he is describing corruption by a different name.[310]

Resistance to the idea of freedom from corruption as a human right derives from the positivist orientation of human rights law. It is said to be difficult to derive or infer such a right from existing human rights instruments. Indeed, the scholars and policymakers who specialize in anti-corruption appear more open to the idea that there is a human right to be free from corruption than human rights scholars themselves.[311] But many anti-corruption activists clearly see freedom from corruption in terms of human rights.

In today's world, persuasive legal arguments are not made by arguing from natural law. Resonating with Spalding's philosophical argument, this monograph, however, provides evidence of anti-corruption movements as manifestations of an alternative source of positive law, theorized through general principles. That would also resolve the dissonance that has emerged between international law, which sees anti-corruption as a matter of criminal law, and people-power campaigns against corruption, which see it as a matter of rights.

Augmenting Natural Law with General Principles

Spalding's approach can be complemented with evidence from nonviolent resistance campaigns against corruption through the general principles approach that this monograph is developing. This approach would look at the anti-corruption activities of people power movements for evidence that they are expressing a demand that can be reflected in general principles identified earlier, namely, nondiscrimination, nonrepression, nonexploitation, and nonviolence. When corruption is seen as depriving people of their "dignity," opposition to corruption may be seen as conceptually aligned with the right to an accountable government and the rights to be free from exploitation and repression, even if it is not yet a human right to which people are legally entitled through positive law. For example, the desire for freedom from corruption may express a grievance that an unaccountable government is behind economic suffering and deprivation, as well as the anxiety, physical and mental ill health created by lack of proper education, reliable health care, unpolluted environment or jobs and economic security. In Tunisia, demonstrators shouted, "jobs are a basic human right, you corruption mafia;" and "no to repression, you government of corruption."[312] Anti-corruption demonstrations around the world have featured calls for governments to step down, from Guatemala's trending hashtag *Renuncia ya* (resign now) to a huge banner being held aloft by a crowd in Brazil calling for the impeachment of President Dilma Rousseff, ensnarled in a corruption scandal. In both Guatemala and Brazil these calls were successful.

Demonstrators demanding the resignation of Brazilian president Dilma Rousseff, March 2016. Source: Naomi Larsson, "Anti-corruption protests around the world – in pictures," *The Guardian*, March 18, 2016. https://www.theguardian.com/global-development-professionals-network/gallery/2016/mar/18/anti-corruption-protests-around-the-world-in-pictures#img-1

Across the globe, anti-corruption activists frame their demands in terms of rights, and the lines between human rights defenders and anti-corruption activists are increasingly blurred. In 2011 in Kenya, a small group of human rights defenders were arrested after staging a sit-in outside the office of the Minister of Education, after an audit report showed that KSh 4.6 billion, some intended to provide free schooling, had gone missing in the Ministry of Education.[313] Protesters in South Africa equated corruption with violations of physical integrity, holding a sign that said, "Corruption is killing us."[314] A grassroots group in the United Kingdom called UK UNKUT has been mobilizing to "highlight alternatives to the government's spending cuts" (UK UNKUT website, 2013) by demonstrating against corporations who are failing to pay their fair share of taxes.[315] A video for the group describes the cuts as "unjust." Disability rights activists argue that they will reduce the care available to disabled persons.[316] The language of rights permeates the discourse of protesters.

In contrast to the difficulty of taming corruption through top-down initiatives from the international level, people-powered resistance efforts have had notable successes. For example, citizens' groups in South Korea, fatigued with governmental corruption and blocked from monitoring the performance of officials in the National Assembly, responded by devising a plan to blacklist the most corrupt politicians and force them from office.[317] Because this plan was in violation of an election law, the action was technically civil disobedience and organizers took the risk of fines and imprisonment into account in devising their strategy. But anger against public corruption was so high that within a short time, a large coalition including 1,104 civic networks and groups emerged and joined the effort.[318] Through a campaign involving a wide variety of tactics, the coalition succeeded with its plan. Worldwide anti-corruption movements have used a variety of such inventive tactics.[319]

Perhaps the greatest successes in combatting corruption thus far have occurred through the combined efforts of top-down global governance initiatives and bottom-up people power. As noted above, top officials in Guatemala, including the president, have resigned and been criminally prosecuted on a variety of corruption charges following massive anti-corruption demonstrations that were held in the spring and summer of 2015. These events were made possible by an extraordinary international-national collaboration that was without precedent in international relations. In late 2006, the government of Guatemala and the UN signed an agreement creating the International Commission Against Impunity in Guatemala (CICIG), an independent commission operating under Guatemalan law with the power to initiate investigations, act as a complementary prosecutor in court proceedings, promote disciplinary administrative processes against any officials, and recommend legal, judicial, and institutional reforms. Because of its backing by the international community and its authorization under Guatemalan law, this commission had the resources and political will to investigate and prosecute corruption at the highest levels of the Guatemalan government. But it took the anti-corruption movement that emerged after the CICIG published its report to force out the top public officials implicated by CICIG. CICIG's achievements are currently being rolled back, thanks in large measure to the lack of support from the Trump administration; but they provide a model of what international-domestic cooperation-driven change could look like.

Takeaway

The cascading global citizen's movements against corruption arguably provide a necessary recognition of and legitimacy for a right to be free of corruption as a general principle of human rights law. To make this argument more conclusive, it will be necessary long-term to have the assistance of researchers and academics, both on the ground and in the universities, to gather evidence of discrete anti-corruption movements, their frequency, intensity, and geographical distribution along with qualitative evidence indicating their resonance with the general principles of nondiscrimination, nonrepression, nonexploitation, and nonviolence. This will demonstrate that a widespread demand for a right to be free of corruption is being raised by mobilized nonviolent movements and is coalescing and exerting coercive effect on elites and institutions.

Right to Democratic Self-Determination

In 1992, Franck advanced the claim that, in the collapse of the Soviet Union and the rise of a pro-democracy movement in China prior to the crackdown in June 1989, the world was witnessing the global triumph of a democratic ideal that was first expressed in the American Declaration of Independence. Through a combination of emerging customary international law and treaty interpretation, "[d]emocracy," Franck argued, "is on the way to becoming a global entitlement," even a condition of a state's recognition in the community of states, "one that increasingly will be promoted and protected by collective international processes."[320] Twenty-five years later, however, this norm still has not consolidated. In fact, the last ten years have seen a strong and surprisingly successful pushback by authoritarian regimes against pro-democracy forces at home and democratic pressure from abroad. A number of established democracies have also seen populist pushback and backsliding toward illiberalism and anti-rule of law practices.

Full explication of the reasons for anti-democratic pushback and backsliding exceeds the scope of this monograph, but those reasons surely include the ramping up of counterterrorism efforts worldwide in the aftermath of September 11th; the impact of globalization and lingering economic consequences of the 2008 Great Recession; and the democratic "Color Revolutions" in what Russia considers its "near-abroad" giving rise to a newly aggressive Russian foreign policy.

Franck's claim that international law was newly developing a "right to democracy" shows that such a right was not yet recognized. International human rights law is somewhat schizophrenic with respect to a right to democracy. The UN Charter does not mention democracy but links human rights and self-determination in Articles 1 and 55, without, however, clearly explicating either term. At the same time, Article 1 of both the ICCPR and ICESCR declares the right of self-determination, defined broadly as a right enabling "peoples" to "freely determine their political status and freely pursue their economic, social and cultural development."[321] By their terms, Article 1 in both Covenants seems to guarantee the right of a people to democratically choose their form of self-government. Article 25 of the ICCPR protects, among other things, the rights "to take part in the conduct of public affairs, directly or through freely chosen representatives" and "to vote and to be elected at genuine periodic elections which shall be by universal and equal suffrage and shall be held by secret ballot, guaranteeing the free expression of the will of the electors."[322] But, as Franck recognized, the "notion that the [international] community can impose such standards, on which the democratic entitlement is based" is in tension with the principle of state sovereignty, embodied in Article 2(7) of the UN Charter, which provides that the UN shall not interfere in matters "essentially within the domestic jurisdiction of states."

Theoretically, consensus on a "right to democracy" was set back in 2001 by the publication of Rawls's influential book, *The Law of Peoples*, in which he argued for a distinction between human rights and democracy. With the purpose of trying to arrive at universal consensus about basic human rights, Rawls argued that it was possible for so-called decent (but non-democratic) states to respect human rights. He argued that the international community can only demand of a state that it actually protects human rights, not that it do so in the form of a particular governance system like democracy.[323] While controversial to some, this idea found a receptive audience among those who feared the coercive interventions that might be unleashed in the name of "democracy," a fear that has come to pass. There has also been some resistance to the idea of a right to democracy coming from scholars and activists from the Global South, who often see democracy as a political form of government imposed by the West that brings along unwelcome economic effects.

In this final section, the monograph takes another approach to the topic of a right to democracy, arguing that a right to democracy can be triggered in the context of a nonviolent movement engaged in a self-determination struggle, irrespective of whether there is a general right to democracy recognized in international law, provided that it meets the criteria set out in Part II above for reflecting a human rights *ethos*.

The theory underlying nonviolent civil resistance teaches that all political power, even the most autocratic, rests on the consent and cooperation of the governed. Thus, as Wilson has argued, a social contract underlies every arrangement of state and governmental power, even though that contract may at times be latent or dormant. This notion of a dormant social contract has implications for the notion of sovereignty in international law. Since international law is state-centric, it does not require that member states in the international system have the actual consent of their population. What is required is the bare minimum of "acquiescence," understood as the absence of open revolt. This bare minimum of acquiescence is all that is required for a government having "effective control" of the population to be recognized by other states in the international system as legitimate.[324] Acquiescence thus carries legal significance. But even when the people have been acquiescing in a particular arrangement of political power over time, the eruption of large-scale nonviolent civil resistance signals that the dormant social contract is being activated, and the people are withdrawing their acquiescence. Arguably, this withdrawal should carry legal significance to the same degree that acquiescence carries legal significance.[325]

Internal struggles for "effective control" are generally viewed in international law as political in nature, not as involving the right of self-determination. Although the UN Charter contains several references to self-determination, a question that was left open in the years after 1945 was whether self-determination was a general principle and applicable to all states, or whether it was limited to colonial situations.[326] The inclusion of Article 1 in both the ICCPR and ICESCR occurred within the de-colonization context and the right of colonialized peoples to throw off colonial rule has never been in doubt. Spain, Portugal and, to a lesser extent, France insisted during the post-WWII period that self-determination did not apply to their territories in Africa because those were not "colonies" but had been integrated into the colonizing mother state and now formed an integral part of that sovereign state.[327] The International Court of Justice initially ratified this view but then quickly backed away from it, confirming that self-determination was a right that colonies could invoke. However, the use of self-determination to legitimate secessionist movements generally and give rise to break-away states outside of the context of colonialism has been sharply circumscribed in international law. And even within the colonial context, the principle of *uti possidetis* (the principle that colonial state boundaries would be maintained even after de-colonization) means that self-determination faces pre-established limits defined by colonialism.

The treaty bodies associated with both the ICCPR and ICESCR have not done much to clarify the meaning of self-determination. The HRC's General Comment on Article 1 is brief and opaque. It calls self-determination a "right," but as Crawford notes, it is "otherwise rather evasive."[328] The tension between self-determination and the principle of

124

nonintervention is unresolved. In practically its only substantive remark regarding the topic, the HRC said that Article 1 imposed "obligations on States parties, not only in relation to their own peoples but vis-à-vis all peoples who have not been able to exercise or have been deprived of the possibility of exercising their right to self-determination," including those peoples who depend on a state not party to the ICCPR.[329] But the HRC simultaneously affirmed the principle of nonintervention: "Such positive action [as states are obligated to take under Article 1] must be consistent with the States' obligations under the Charter of the UN and under international law: in particular, *States must refrain from interfering in the internal affairs of other States and thereby adversely affecting the exercise of the right to self-determination*" (italics added).[330] Noting that many state parties did not address Article 1 in their reports, the HRC enjoined states parties to "describe the constitutional and political processes which in practice allow the exercise of this right," without giving guidance as to what processes should be reported.[331]

In practical terms, after the process of de-colonialization was largely completed (with the sole exception of Western Sahara), the "self-determination of peoples" has been generally understood as applying to peoples within sovereign, non-colonial states, with its main application being with respect to minority peoples within those states and their rights to internal self-determination or relatively autonomous self-governance. With respect to the "people" of the state as a whole, self-determination has largely been interpreted in terms of the exercise of democratic rights like freedom of expression and political participation, not to the process of democratization as such.

There is a question why this should be so. If self-determination applies to all "peoples," as it does by the terms of the treaties, and not just to "minority peoples," then it should also apply to political self-determination within nation states. In fact, as a historical matter, the notion of self-determination was first born as a political concept, the result of nationalist movements during the 19th century. That was a period of simultaneous nation-state consolidation and democratic revolution, where "the people" and not the king began to say, "l'état, c'est moi" (I am the state). But with respect to majority peoples, self-determination has remained a political principle, not a legal one.

Takeaway

It is arguable that when a people is mobilized through large-scale nonviolent resistance, it is in effect withdrawing its consent from the governing political arrangement of power, activating a dormant social contract, and exercising its right to self-determination. Put another way, a large-scale assertion of civil resistance is in effect shifting the locus of sovereignty from the state to the people. Since it is sovereignty that gives states the lawmaking power that they alone, as subjects of international law, are thought to have, this shift in the locus of sovereignty (from state to people) should carry with it at least some lawmaking power as well, vested now in a nonviolently mobilized population demanding specific rights.

International legal scholars may object that what is happening in such a scenario is that the people are withdrawing their consent from the government, not the state, and under international law, it is the state that is sovereign, not the government. International law makes a clear distinction between governments and states. Governments come and go, but the state remains. For good reason, the international community has a preference for inertia when it comes to state formation. However, the distinction between state and government rests on the legal fiction of "the state," which is dependent on the will of the international community. A state can declare its own existence, but if it is not recognized by other states, it will have difficulty functioning as a state. Once the international community decides that its will is to recognize a state, it is very difficult for that state to go out of existence, as the international community will work to keep the fiction of the state alive. This is what happened with respect to Germany after the Second World War. The collapse of the German government and the partition of Germany into four sectors could have signaled the end of the particular political arrangement called the state of Germany. But pragmatically, it would not have done anything to resolve the instability in the heart of Europe to incorporate German-speaking peoples into neighboring states, which would have been the logical alternative. Consequently, the Allies announced that they had no intention of acquiring German territory and that the sovereignty of the state remained. Similar considerations of maintaining state integrity are going into the refusal of most states in the international system to recognize Somaliland as a new and separate state, as such recognition would negate the continued existence of Somalia, even though Somaliland is more functioning and state-like than the rest of Somalia at present.

The state that is the lawmaker in international law is a fictional state, an idea that is sustained by the international community. The actual state on the ground can "fail" and the distinction between state and government may become blurred, especially when the head of the government is simultaneously the "head of state" and carries immunity that derives from the state's sovereignty. Similarly, in some cases, the organized corruption that people oppose is embedded in the state structure and is not a product of one or another government. If the international community can evolve a system of norms that endows the state with a fictional existence that can survive the dissolution of the government and displacement of the people, it can also find a way for norm evolution that recognizes and respects the organized withdrawal of consent of people from their government. It only needs to find the will—and the appropriate intellectual justification—to do so. This monograph takes the first step in creating that justification.

That the right of self-determination is set out in not one but two human rights treaties implies that we should interpret it in the light of the rest of the language of each of those treaties as a whole, per the interpretive principles of the Vienna Convention on the Law of Treaties. Reading the right of self-determination in light of the other human rights set out in the ICCPR and ICESCR leads to the conclusion that large-scale people power movements that respect the general principles of human rights can be said to have a legal entitlement to democracy. This right to democracy may not create a duty as a matter of positive law on the part of other *states* to assist nonviolent activists in their struggles for democratic self-determination because of the norm of nonintervention and the fact that interventions can do more harm than good. But it would accord with the general (natural law) principles of human rights to say that *non-state actors* committed to the human rights project have both a right and a duty to do everything in their power to help those engaged in such struggles achieve their objectives.

IN CONCLUSION

Takeaways of the Monograph Findings for Various Constituents

*T*he analysis in this monograph is premised on the belief that civil resistance practitioners and researchers, and human rights legal scholars and activists stand to gain if closer theoretical and practical relations between them are forged and mutual understanding is improved.

The idea of human rights carries a high degree of prestige and respect among both scholars, policy makers, and the public and has given rise to a broad array of institutions. Civil resistance movements, in contrast, remain poorly understood by policy makers and by scholars outside of the exciting and growing subject area of civil resistance studies. Showing that civil resistance movements can, and often do, manifest human rights norms can lend them some of the prestige of human rights, legitimizing and enhancing the status of civil resistance movements.

At the same time, the human rights project is facing pessimistic appraisals about its achievements. Even though human rights ideals are respected, international human rights mechanisms are frequently criticized for being elite, top-down institutions that have no real purchase on the grassroots.[332] Understanding how bottom-up civil resistance movements reflect and further human rights can help the human rights project rebut the criticism that its concerns do not resonate "on the ground."

What is in the Monograph for Legal and Other Scholars

For legal scholars, the central contribution this monograph makes is to develop a non-state-centric approach—specifically, a *demos*-centric perspective—to international human rights law. The aim is to take account of the actions of individuals (acting alone or in association) in accordance with certain general principles of human rights that crosscut international and domestic law, as well as positive and natural law, and that define a human rights *ethos*. Because they may be derived from natural law, general principles have traditionally been viewed as expressing morality, the conscience of a legal community, broadly defined. This monograph goes, however, further and argues that general principles can be created and embodied by the activities of organized nonviolent individuals, not only by states. The key originality of the monograph lies in how it rehabilitates natural law by "operationalizing" it as collective practice, treating the organized activities of mobilized individuals as practice that becomes legally relevant to the determination of human rights law as a kind of analogy to state practice, to the extent that such activities are designed and executed consistent with the overall general principles that characterize the human rights *ethos*. In that way, this monograph argues, a second, even alternative, source of legal meaning is created that is independent of, though to some extent parallel to, the state practice that traditionally shaped the emergence and applicability of human rights norms. This monograph thus opens a theoretical and conceptual door for a *demos*-centric perspective to play a significant and concrete role in shaping and even determining new human rights norms.

The monograph creates an interdisciplinary research agenda for future collaboration between legal scholars and social scientists. Scholars of civil resistance studies can be attentive to evidence that the civil resistance movements they study are manifesting a human rights *ethos*. Legal scholars can evaluate this evidence and incorporate it into developing and strengthening general principles of human rights law, ensuring conceptual consistency across different dimensions of law and recognizing the potential of civil resistance movements to aid in the "internalization" of international law into domestic legal systems and to push both international and domestic law in new directions.

Another facet of this collaborative research agenda concerns incorporating research regarding the human rights *bone fides* of civil resistance into research on the effectiveness of human rights generally. A distortion in empirical scholarship on human rights has arisen because of an unnecessarily narrow focus on legal frameworks imposed by the dominant positive-law focused approach to international human rights. The skeptical question was first posed by Oona Hathaway in a particularly important early quantitative study, "Do human rights treaties make a difference?" In responses to this question, it is frequently observed that the added value of human rights law is dubious because of an overlap with the more general process of democratization:[333]

"[The] past three decades have been an era of widespread democratization... Since many of the rights contained in the ICCPR are practically synonymous with democracy, it is difficult to show that practices are influenced—at least in part—by an international treaty commitment as distinct from these broader processes."[334] The assumption in such law-focused human rights research is that democratization and international treaties are "distinct processes," even though they in fact advance similar rights.

But why should studies on the effectiveness of human rights be narrowly confined to the added value of human rights treaties? Because of the "effective control" doctrine when it comes to the recognition of governments and states, international legal scholars have seldom studied, or taken account of, pro-democracy nonviolent movements. But this monograph has begun to show that pro-democracy people power movements may be motivated by, integrate, or reflect, the general principles of human rights norms. While it is probably true that international law played a relatively small role in pro-democratic nonviolent movements, human rights principles may be internalized and advanced by such movements. Such principles may contribute to shaping movement goals, as well as domestic discourse about human rights and the place of those rights in the future post-revolutionary constitutional order. It undercounts the influence of the human rights idea to confine the analysis to the effects of positive international law based on state practices.

A people-powered approach will not solve the problem of a generally applicable law of human rights that all states respect to the same degree that they respect settled aspects of customary law (assuming that such settled aspects actually exist). But it may go some way toward allaying the anxiety about the absence of a generally applicable law among international lawyers. We are not losing anything in starting to think of people power as a source of human rights, since we have never had a generally applicable positive law of human rights to begin with. And by thinking of people power as the true source of human rights, what we (fictitiously) lose in state compliance, we can make up by closing the democratic deficit. Taking account of people power in the formation and implementation of international human rights law puts agency into the hands of the supposed beneficiaries of human rights law and acknowledges that they are the original source of human rights. In fact, recognition of people power can help to overcome the central weakness of the international law—namely, its inability to ensure compliance of states and governments with the obligations they supposedly undertake.

Except for treaties, which have existed from time immemorial, "international law" does not emerge purely from the practice of states in consenting to it.[335] It emerges from the dialectical relationship between the emergence of a certain pattern of organizing relations on a global, or at least a regional scale, and an intellectual justification that both describes that order and generates rules for its maintenance and evolution. Critically minded international lawyers could direct themselves to analyzing the extent to which the ideology of state-centric international law has contributed to human rights violations committed in the name of the state's "survival."[336] Such an analysis would have to be counterbalanced by recognition that the "pure" state system of 19th-century international law gave way to the modern system where a web of international organizations, primarily the UN, constrains and moderates state "survivalism," although this system is being pressured by the current authoritarian backlash. The nation-state system is a historical phase, perhaps one that has attained a certain stability and power to endure, but at this point it is arguably failing the most important test confronting the international community at the present time—the threat of climate change. It is not certain whether growing climate change movements and campaigns will succeed in forcing states, particularly major state polluters, to recognize the urgency of the moment. If the state-centric system fails to respond adequately to this catastrophic threat to human existence, we may see the end of the state-based system we have now and a transition to a new, probably more primitive pattern of organized human relations characterized by chaos, violence, and suffering.

What is in the Monograph for Civil Resisters

Strengthening how civil resistance movements may be understood in relation to the international human rights project will make it easier for activists to understand the vital role that their movements may have to play in realizing human rights and even expanding them beyond existing legal frameworks and political practices. Aligning civil resistance efforts with the international human rights project can make such movements more legible for society, other states and the international community, in terms of their goals and relation to formal legal frameworks and institutions.

Nonviolent civil resisters may find it advantageous to educate themselves about applicable human rights norms and seek out ways to leverage international human rights mechanisms when it may be advantageous to do so. To the extent that nonviolent civil resisters can translate their demands (if contextually appropriate) into terms utilized by international human rights law, it will be easier for those demands to be understood, seen as less threatening and more legitimate. Nonviolent activists may find that using the discourse of "rights" is unifying, helping and strengthening their efforts in coalition-building across different segments of the society and may help a movement gather ground, as occurred in communist Poland a few decades ago or in Ukraine in recent years.

Although grassroots organizations may have good reason to be suspicious of elite-driven international CSOs, it is important to be aware that potent synergies can be created when elite and grassroots organizations work in tandem, as was the case in Argentina in the late 1980s and in Guatemala in the 2010s.

Using the general principles—nonexploitation, nondiscrimination, nonrepression, and nonviolence—may even be helpful to practitioners of nonviolent civil resistance in strengthening nonviolent discipline, avoiding Trojan horses, and in successfully steering a movement to more democratic, long-term outcomes. Activists may want to make a greater determination to engage in long-term constructive programs such as education and parallel institution building, in order to be better prepared should they actually be successful in their campaigns and need to take power.

What is in the Monograph for International and Local CSOs and their Representatives

The analysis in this monograph may help to enhance mutual understanding between the traditional world of human rights CSOs and more grassroots-oriented people power movements, between which there may exist mutual suspicion or misunderstandings. Though the abstract ideals of human rights seem to have wide appeal, grassroots nonviolent movements may elicit more mixed reactions from policy makers and analysts. Yet the analysis in this monograph indicates that civil resistance movements may be both useful and powerful partners for international human rights organizations and networks and can play an important role in realizing human rights through internalization in domestic law. Civil resistance movements can encompass and access local grassroots activists and organizations that more elite international human rights organizations may not have the capacity, including on-the-ground legitimacy, to reach.

f the general principles outlined in this monograph are taken seriously, CSOs have a right to resist oppression and a duty to assist others in resisting oppression. This duty falls primarily to civil society, since non-state actors are not constrained by the norm of nonintervention that dictates states not to interfere in the domestic activities of other states. At this point, this duty is a matter of natural law, not positive law.

CSOs could aid in the development of customary international law applicable to the right of peaceful protest by including in shadow reports submitted to the UNHRC as part of the UPR process, accounts of how well states have respected the recommendations in the Joint Report when responding to peaceful assemblies. They could also identify the extent to which legitimate grassroots forces of ordinary men and women, embodying general principles as identified in this monograph, are present on the ground, as well as the frequency and potency by which those grassroots forces continue nonviolent struggles to advance specific rights.

Civil society practitioners have further reasons to become more informed about nonviolent civil resistance. In many countries around the world today, local civil society practitioners are working in difficult environments. Authoritarianism has been resurgent. Dictators are learning from one another how to "close the space" in which traditional CSOs operate. In many cases, this is being done through "legal" means: restrictive laws that are designed to make it almost impossible for CSOs to get licenses, receive foreign funding, or conduct other day-to-day operations. In other cases, their activities are criminalized, or as in Russia, human rights-related CSOs are required to register as foreign agents.

The closing of space for traditional civil society means that human rights defenders and CSOs that work in such repressive environments find themselves being drained of resources, their voices stifled, and their reputations stained. They may find that they will increasingly have to coordinate with activists who employ the "lawless" methods of nonviolent resistance, and perhaps fall back on such methods themselves. For example, in 2009, Ethiopia adopted a particularly draconian law cracking down on CSOs, the Charities and Societies Proclamation (No. 621/2009). It is perhaps not surprising that various forms of nonviolent defiance—symbolic resistance, marches and demonstrations, and call for boycotts—have taken place in Ethiopia with increasing intensity since 2015, as more legalized modes of resistance have been choked off.

What is in the Monograph for the International Community

The analysis in this monograph gives the international community additional intellectual rationale for incorporating popular sovereignty into the principles uncerlying the international legal order and creating a *demos*-centric approach to sovereignty in international law. The past two decades saw the rise—and arguable fall—of the responsibility to protect (R2P), which was initially a celebrated attempt to reformulate sovereignty in international law and make it more congruent with the view increasingly dominant in domestic legal systems that sovereignty resides in the people. Most famous for articulating a standard for guiding humanitarian interventions, R2P at its core was an attempt to reformulate how sovereignty is understood in international law, shifting from a perspective stressing the state's authority to one emphasizing the state's respor sibility. Its rapid development at the international level responded to the pained query of former UN Secretary-General Kofi Annan in the Millennial Report of 2000: "If humanitarian intervention is, indeed, an unacceptable assault on sovereignty, how should we respond to a Rwanda, to a Srebrenica, to gross and systematic violation of human rights that offend every precept of our common humanity?"[337] Annan's question gave rise to the report of the International Commission on Intervention and State Sovereignty (ICISS). As paraphrased in the ICISS Report, the Secretary-General posed "the dilemma in the conceptual language of two notions of sovereignty, one vesting in the state, the second in the people and in individuals."[338]

As should be evident from the foregoing analysis, the idea of reformulating state sovereignty so that it emphasizes the responsibility of the state to "protect" its citizens still rests on a paternalistic view that state power inheres in the state itself and not in its people.[339] "Responsibility" in this sense is a kind of *noblesse oblige* that the state may choose to exercise, not a right to which the people are entitled, as opposed to say accountability, in which the state must answer to its constituents. The ICISS Report noted that Annan's approach "reflects the ever-increasing commitment around the world to democratic government (of, by and for the people) and greater popular freedoms," but it did not note that this notion of sovereignty as vested in the people is a notion of sovereignty confined to domestic legal systems exclusively. International law vests sovereignty only in the state, and R2P with its paternalist invocation of "protection" did little to change that.

Since international organizations like the UN are by definition state-centric, mainly recognizing non-state actors through the consultative status granted to certain qualifying CSOs, such organizations will have a certain structural resistance to putting human beings at the center of international law. Within international organizations, individuals who are interested in promoting human rights may have to think creatively about how they might shift the focus from cajoling states to comply with their human rights obligations to recognizing and empowering citizens to realize their rights through nonviolent struggle. The case of CICIG and people power in Guatemala can be a model.

Third-party states can also promote a *demos*-centric approach in their practice. As an example, the US government recently prosecuted a "kleptocracy" case against the Second Vice-President of Equatorial Guinea, Teodoro Nguema Obiang Mangue, who had purchased lavish real estate and other luxury goods in the United States with millions of dollars stolen from the people of Equatorial Guinea. As part of the settlement, Obiang Mangue was required to give $20 million to a charity for his own people, to begin to compensate them for the money that was stolen from them.

GLOSSARY OF TERMS

Civil resistance movements or campaigns: This monograph uses the following definition of "movement" put forward by Hardy Merriman. A movement is understood as:

"Ongoing collective efforts aimed at bringing about consequential change in a social, economic or political order. Movements are civilian-based, involve widespread popular participation, and alert, educate, serve, and mobilize people in order to create change."[340]

At times, when referring to concrete examples of organized and sustained collective actions undertaken as part of a larger movement or struggle, this monograph uses the term "campaign," as defined in Chenoweth and Stephan's, *Why Civil Resistance Works:*

"a series of observable, continuous, purposive mass tactics or events in pursuit of a political objective. Campaigns are observable, meaning that the tactics used are overt and documented. A campaign is continuous and lasts anywhere from days to years, distinguishing it from one-off events or revolts. Campaigns are also purposive, meaning that they are consciously acting with a specific objective in mind, such as expelling a foreign occupier or overthrowing a domestic regime. Campaigns have discernible leadership and often have names, distinguishing them from random riots or spontaneous mass acts."[341]

Civil Rights: Usually refers to rights that are guaranteed by the positive laws in domestic legal systems, often in constitutions. Civil rights may overlap with human rights and be a way that international law is implemented in the domestic law of the land. However, civil rights may be different from—less or more protective than—human rights.

Civil society: The formal and informal voluntary associations that exist in a polity outside of the state and the for-profit sector.

Civil society organizations (CSOs): Formal or informal organizations through which individuals associate in order to carry out the day-to-day work of defending human rights. These can be domestic (e.g. Helsinki Committee in communist Poland or Human Rights Center 'Memorial' in Russia), regional, or international (Human Rights Watch, Amnesty International), incorporated or unincorporated, registered or unregistered. Typically, these organizations support work, directly or indirectly, for the international legal frameworks through such activities as education and monitoring.

General Assembly: The main representative body of the United Nations (UN), to which all member states send representatives.

General Principles of International Law: The third "source" of international law (see entry "Sources of Law") after international agreements and custom. General principles as a source of law refers to common doctrines or modes of reasoning found at multiple levels of the international system, or in a wide number of domestic legal systems, or in natural law.

Human rights defenders or activists: Individuals who work to realize human rights, either alone or through associating with others. According to Article 1 of the Declaration on the Right and Responsibility of Individuals, Groups, and Organs of Society to Promote and Protect Universally Recognized Human Rights and Fundamental Freedoms ("Declaration on Human Rights Defenders" or "DHRD"):[342]

> To be a human rights defender, a person can act to address any human right (or rights) on behalf of individuals or groups. Human rights defenders seek the promotion and protection of civil and political rights as well as the promotion, protection and realization of economic, social and cultural rights.

Human rights project: The term used in this monograph to refer to the collective project of realizing human rights. It includes legal mechanisms (treaties, treaty monitoring bodies, regional human rights courts, UN special procedures, committees and agencies); education and culture; social movements; as well as intellectual work (history, theory, and social science). The "human rights project" is what Michel Foucault might call a "discursive formation."

Jurisgenesis: Term coined by the legal scholar Robert M. Cover to designate the process of creation of legal meaning by social groups within a society.

Jus cogens: Norms of international law considered so fundamental, grave, and important that their violation admits no justification. Small in number, *jus cogens* norms include slavery, Apartheid, and first use of force.

Modern (or instant) custom: A term used to describe scholarly efforts to reconceptualize customary international law, primarily in order to make it a more accurate description of how human rights form customary norms. The main approaches emphasize the element of "*opinio juris*" over that of state practice.

Natural law: According to Black's Law Dictionary, natural law is a "philosophical system of legal principles purportedly deriving from a universalized conception of human nature or divine justice rather than from legislative or judicial action."

Nonviolent civil resistance, nonviolent resistance or civil resistance: This monograph uses the following definition of nonviolent civil resistance. Nonviolent resistance is a civilian-based method used to wage conflict through social, psychological, economic, and political means without the threat or use of violence. It includes acts of omission, acts of commission, or a combination of both. Scholars have identified hundreds of nonviolent methods—including symbolic protests, economic boycotts, labor strikes, political and social noncooperation, and nonviolent intervention—that groups have used to mobilize publics to oppose or support different policies, to delegitimize adversaries, and to remove or restrict adversaries' sources of power.[343]

Opinio juris: One of the two elements of customary law, the other being a consistent and widespread pattern of state practice. It refers to a sense of legal obligation that accompanies state practice, meaning that the state is behaving in a particular way because it believes it is legally obligated to behave in that way.

Peaceful protest: This is a term increasingly used in international law, particularly in the context of the UN, to designate the amalgamated right of an individual or group to peacefully assemble and express their political opinions.

People power: The term "people power" was initially coined during the large-scale civil resistance movement to remove Philippine dictator Ferdinand Marcos in 1986 and install a democratic alternative. Although originally signifying large-scale pro-democracy movements, the term is now used more generally to refer to campaigns of any size that use the techniques of civil resistance.[344] It will be used in this monograph interchangeably with civil resistance movements or campaigns, or simply, civil resistance to describe or illustrate the same phenomenon. It should also be noted, however, that people power – as the socially-articulated agency of individuals acting alone or in association – also encompasses both the active and passive means through which individuals create, sustain, and dismantle political arrangements of power. The former includes the social contract (agreement to be ruled over in exchange for safety, security and personal freedom); the dormant social contract (that connotes everyday obedience practice that became routinized even though rulers do not keep their side of the deal) as well as the social contract renunciation moment (when people activize the spirit and letter of social contract by asserting their right to remove rulers that do not fulfil their part of the social contract obligations). Such understanding of people power is thus potentially much broader than the traditional definition or meaning of nonviolent resistance.

Positive law: In contrast to natural law, which is often seen as being divine in origin, positive law designates man-made law. In the context of international law, this refers to law emerging from the practice of states belonging to the international community, whether written or unwritten, whether codified or not.

Source of Law: In international law, a source of law is the source of legal authority. There is no "legislator" in international law, so the sources of law lie in international agreements, the customs of states, and general principles.

State and Non-State Actors: International law recognizes two main types of actors—state and non-state. States are the entities formally recognized in the international legal order. Though recognition of states occurs through the process of diplomatic relations among states, it is formalized mainly through membership in the UN.[345] Non-state actors are everyone else—individuals, insurgent groups, terrorist organizations, chambers of commerce, environmental advocacy groups, and civil resistance movements, among others.

Subjects and objects of international law: Legal scholars generally use the term "subjects" to designate actors having legal personality in international law and "objects" to designate those that do not. An entity is recognized as having "international legal personality" if it is capable of exercising rights or duties under international law. In the past, individuals were considered "objects" of international law, because they had no rights and duties under international law and could not "invoke it for... protection nor violate its rules." They were "things," like real property or natural resources, with their relationship to international law mediated through the state.[346] Today, individuals are considered "subjects" of international law because they are both rights-holders and duty-bearers. They possess a wide array of human rights, and they have the more limited duty of not committing international crimes like genocide and ethnic cleansing. However, non-state actors do not have law-making power. International law does not have a separate term to distinguish subjects having law-making powers from subjects not having law-making powers, though one would be useful.

United Nations Human Rights Council (UNHRC): The body within the UN tasked with monitoring compliance of member states with the human rights provisions of the UN Charter, mainly through the UPR process. The UNHRC was formed in 2008 when its predecessor body, the Human Rights Commission, was dissolved.

APPENDIX: A BRIEF INTRODUCTION TO THE POSITIVE LAW OF HUMAN RIGHTS

This appendix provides a basic introduction to international law for the benefit of readers who are not lawyers or otherwise knowledgeable about the subject, with a particular focus on human rights law.

A. *What international law is*

International law is the body of rules and principles of general application dealing with the conduct of states and of international organizations, and with their relations among themselves, as well as with some of their relations with natural persons (human beings) or legal persons (e.g., CSOs or corporations).[347] Unlike domestic law, international law is not created by a central legislative body, though the UN, especially the Security Council, sometimes plays a role akin to a legislature. Nor is there a central executive or enforcement mechanism. In contrast to domestic law, which is created through legislative or executive authority and is set out in statutes and constitutions, international law takes a different form and has four main sources, which are set out in Article 38 of the Statute of the ICJ. The two most important and least controversial sources of international law are 1) "international conventions, whether general or particular" and 2) "international custom" (also known as customary law). A third source is "the general principles of law recognized by civilized nations." "[J]udicial decisions and the teachings of the most highly qualified publicists of the various nations" may also be consulted "as subsidiary means" for determining rules of law."[348]

1.) *International agreements*

International agreements, or "conventional law," refer to treaties or other agreements that are negotiated between or among states. Treaties are like contracts between states: according to their specific terms, they create obligations for the states that sign onto them. Rules for the interpretation of treaties are set out in the Vienna Convention on the Law of Treaties, which is a codification of the customary law regarding the interpretation of treaties. Some rules for interpreting treaties remain uncodified.

2.) International custom or customary law

Whereas conventional law only obligates the specific states that are parties to the specific treaties in question, customary law is generally binding on all states, except those states that are "persistent objectors" to the formation of a particular customary rule and made their objection known to the international community. The law of the sea and the laws of war are prime examples of customary law. In these critical areas, states needed to work out rules so that they would not come into conflict, or if they did come into conflict, the conflict would have some predictability and limits.

The general understanding of customary international law is that it "results from a general and consistent practice of states followed by them from a sense of legal obligation."[349] Customary law is unwritten originally (though it may be later codified into international treaties) and is identified through an inductive process examining the consistent practices that states evolve over time to regularize their interactions with other states and then ascertaining whether those practices are undertaken from a belief that they are in fact legally obliged. An example of a customary rule is that of the "territorial sea"—the rule that states have jurisdiction over the seas and oceans that immediately surround them for reasons of national security and welfare. Respect for the territorial sea was first undertaken for matters of practicality, diplomatic relations, comity, or other reasons, but as it recurred over time, it took on a sense of legal obligation, whereby states conformed their behavior to what was perceived to be a legal rule. When conformity with a regular practice is undertaken out of a "sense of legal obligation," it is said that customary international law has formed. This "sense" of "obligation" is often designated by the Latin term *opinio juris*.

Because it is reciprocal and interactive, customary law can evolve over time as states change their practices and, in turn, their sense of their legal obligations. Customary law also has the unusual feature of change necessarily first appearing as a violation of law; but if an initial violation is followed by many violations, a new law may form. In the case of the territorial sea, for many years the legal limit was set at three nautical miles, but in the mid-20th century, some states "violated" this custom, claiming a territorial sea of 12 nautical miles. When enough states claimed a 12-mile limit, a new customary law was formed.

3.) General principles of law

Although the ICJ Statute puts general principles on the same level with custom and treaty, there is less consensus about what they mean, and some scholars regard them as subsidiary sources of law that are primarily interpretive. The ICJ Statute also qualifies general principles with the phrase "recognized by civilized nations," which many decolonized countries saw as reflecting Eurocentric bias. Today, the phrase is generally assumed to be redundant, meaning nothing more than membership in the international community.

Subjects of international law

A variety of actors, including states, supranational collectives (like the European Union), international organizations, corporations and individuals, are now recognized as having "legal personality" in international law, meaning that international legal frameworks recognize them as "subjects" (see Glossary), with certain rights and duties. However, not all subjects recognized by international law are recognized equally. States have the greatest number of rights, duties and powers while international organizations and individuals have fewer. States remain the only subjects in international law with lawmaking power (which they may sometimes delegate to international organizations).

Though previously considered "objects" of international law, without any legal status, individuals are today considered "subjects" of international law because they are both rights-holders and (to a more limited extent) duty-bearers. As human beings, they are the beneficiaries of the body of law called human rights law, and they enjoy a wide array of rights called human rights. They have the more limited duties of not committing international crimes like genocide, war crimes, and ethnic cleansing. They are exhorted to respect the human rights of others, but through the doctrine of due diligence, states have the prime duty to ensure that individuals respect the human rights of other individuals.[350] Though "subjects" in the sense of having rights and duties, individuals do not have the power to make international law. It would thus be more accurate to consider them "subject-objects" of international law. Since they are composed of individuals, civil resistance movements are likewise not currently recognized as having the legal capacity to make international law, though participants in such movements are rights-holders just like any individuals. In particular, individuals engaged in collective civil resistance are exercising their rights to peaceful assembly and association.

B. International human rights law

International human rights law is the subset of international law that sets forth the obligations that states have to respect the human rights of all persons located within their territory, or affected by their actions abroad. The legally binding UN Charter contains seven references to human rights, and ensuring human rights is one of the stated purposes of the UN. International human rights law currently functions in large measure in the same way that general international law functions, except that the idea of human rights—the notion that human beings have certain basic rights by virtue of their humanity—is considered by some to be a natural law idea.

Instruments of international human rights

The positive law of international human rights is embedded mainly through a network of multilateral (multiparty) treaties. At the origin point of this network is the UDHR, a non-binding General Assembly Resolution adopted in 1948, which sets out an array of rights as "a common standard of achievement for all peoples and all nations."[351] Included in this declaration are civil and political rights, like the rights to "life, liberty and security of person" (Art. 3) and "equal protection of the law" (Art. 7), as well as social, economic, and cultural rights, like "the right to form and join trade unions" (Art. 23) and "the right to education" (Art. 26).

The UDHR was eventually codified in two binding international treaties: the International Covenant of Civil and Political Rights (ICCPR)[352] and the International Covenant of Social, Economic, and Cultural Rights (ICESCR).[353] As its name indicates, the ICCPR protects civil and political rights, like the right of association and expression; the right to information; the right to peaceful assembly; freedom of thought and belief; the right to be secure from unlawful searches and from arbitrary arrest and imprisonment; as well as the right not to be tortured or summarily executed. The ICESCR protects the social, economic, and cultural rights of individuals, including the right to education, the right to health, and the right to join trade unions.

In addition to these three core instruments, the UDHR, the ICCPR, and the ICESCR (often referred to as an "International Bill of Rights"), there are specialized treaties addressing specific rights, or specific groups of rights-holders, that have been deemed to require special attention, such as the Convention Against Torture or the Convention on the Elimination of Discrimination Against Women. While these treaties operate at the global level and have states parties from all geographical regions of the world, there are also regional human rights mechanisms. The European Court of Human Rights and the Inter-American Court of Human Rights are tied to regional human rights conventions—the European Convention on Human Rights and Fundamental Freedoms (European Convention) and the American Convention on Human Rights (American Convention). Such regional treaties may secure rights in overlapping fashion to international treaties, or protect additional rights or other, enhanced means of enforcement.

Enforcement of international human rights

In general, the enforcement mechanisms that international human rights law provides are weak, relying mainly on the moral power of "naming and shaming." Most human rights treaties are administered by an oversight committee made up of independent experts (treaty bodies). In the case of some treaties, like the ICCPR, the state party may choose to sign onto an Optional Protocol that gives individuals the ability to initiate claims on their own. Depending on the specific treaty, the treaty body may have the authority to initiate in-state investigations, but no treaty body has the coercive power to enforce its judgments.

Oversight of the human rights records of UN member states is entrusted to the UNHRC, which has various "special procedures" at its disposal and can designate "special rapporteurs" on either thematic or country-specific topics. These special rapporteurs work to clarify the law and ensure state compliance, through exhortation and other forms of pressure. Since 1993, the human rights activities of the UN have been coordinated by the High Commissioner for Human Rights. The UNHRC has also instituted the Universal Periodic Review (UPR), whereby every member state in the UN undergoes peer review in an open hearing, and civil society is able to participate and submit "shadow reports" that present dissenting opinions and evidence to supplement and sometimes contradict the "official" state reports.[354] The UPR process is "naming and shaming" that occurs at a state-to-state level.

The most effective human rights enforcement mechanisms are found at the regional level. Both the European and Inter-American human rights regimes created juridical systems, including a commission and a court,[355] and both give individuals the right to file petitions. Although these juridical systems have no police powers, many of the state parties to the European and American Conventions have consented to treat their decisions as legally binding and to comply with the respective courts' decisions, which often includes the payment of compensation to victims. However, both regimes are more effective in compelling states to provide compensation for victims than in changing their policies.

ENDNOTES

[1] This monograph was largely written before full scope of right-wing ultra-nationalist populism—more precisely authoritarianism—spreading globally was evident. This darkens the current prospects for the human rights project but does not invalidate the analysis. The current resurgence of authoritarianism has been enabled by a systematic and in many cases legalistic assault on human rights defenders and human rights civil society organizations. See Elizabeth A. Wilson, "National Laws Restricting Foreign Funding of Human Rights Civil Society Organizations: A Legal Analysis," *Journal of Human Rights Practice* 8 (2016): 329-357. Since the human rights project is created by human activity, it can potentially be destroyed by human activity as well. The general principles that nonviolent human rights movements uphold have to be constantly reaffirmed through the *praxis* of ongoing human rights work at every level of international and domestic existence in order for their promise to be fulfilled.

[2] Martin Luther King Jr., "I've Been to the Mountaintop," (speech at the Mason Temple, Memphis, Tennessee, April 3, 1968).

[3] Mohja Kahf, "Nonviolent Resistance by Syrian Women," (presentation at the ICNC Summer Institute, Fletcher School, Tufts University Medford, Massachusetts, USA, June 19, 2014); see also Maciej J. Bartkowski and Mohja Kahf, "The Syrian Resistance: a Tale of Two Struggles," openDemocracy, https://www.opendemocracy.net/civilresistance/maciej-bartkowski-mohja-kahf/syrian-resistance-tale-of-two-struggles.

[4] Erica Chenoweth and Maria J. Stephan, "Why Civil Resistance Works: The Strategic Logic of Nonviolent Conflict," *International Security* 33 (2008), 9-10.

[5] As of 2016, the Westlaw database with more than 40,000 entries for legal research contained only two articles with 10 or more references to "people power," both about the Philippines.

[6] Thomas Carothers and Richard Youngs, *The Complexities of Global Protests* (Carnegie Endowment for International Peace, October 8, 2015), 3.

[7] Ibid.

[8] Ibid.

[9] Erica Chenoweth and Maria J. Stephan, "How the World is Proving Martin Luther King Right about Nonviolence," *Washington Post: Monkey Cage* (blog), January 18, 2016. https://www.washingtonpost.com/news/monkey-cage/wp/2016/01/18/how-the-world-is-proving-mlk-right-about-nonviolence/.

[10] Carothers and Youngs, *Complexities of Global Protests*, 6.

[11] Chenoweth and Stephan, "How the World is Proving Martin Luther King Right about Nonviolence."

[12] In-depth examination of nonviolent resistance in historical independence struggles can be found in Maciej Bartkowski ed., *Recovering Nonviolent History: Civil Resistance in Liberation Struggles* (Boulder: Lynne Rienner Publishers, 2013).

[13] Erica Chenoweth and Maria J. Stephan, *Why Civil Resistance Works: The Strategic Logic of Nonviolent Conflict* (New York: Columbia University Press, 2011), 8. *Why Civil Resistance Works* was the winner of the 2012 Woodrow Wilson Foundation Award from the American Political Science Association and the 2013 University of Louisville Grawemeyer Award for Ideas Improving World Order

[14] Ibid, 30 (noting "a critical source of the success of nonviolent movements is mass participation"); see also ibid, ch. 2, "The Primacy of Participation in Nonviolent Resistance."

[15] In the EuroMaidan protests in Ukraine, one study found that 35% of participants were under the age of 24, 30% were middle-aged professionals with families, and 12% were retired and grandparents. Olga Onuch, "EuroMaidan Protests in Ukraine: Social Media Versus Social Networks," *Problems of Post-Communism* 62 (2015), 217, 222.

[16] Chenoweth and Stephan, *Why Civil Resistance Works,* 66.

[17] See, e.g., UNHRC Res. 19/35, The Promotion and Protection of Human Rights in the Context of Peaceful Protests, 19th Sess., April 18, 2012; UNHRC Res. 22/10, The Promotion and Protection of Human Rights in the Context of Peaceful Protests, 22th Sess., April 9, 2013; UNHRC Res. 25/38, The Promotion and Protection of Human Rights in the Context of Peaceful Protests, 25th Sess., April 11, 2014; see also UNHRC, Summary of the Human Rights Council Panel Discussion on the Promotion and Protection of Human Rights in the Context of Peaceful Protests Prepared by the Office of the United Nations High Commissioner for Human Rights, para. 45, UN Doc. A/HRC/19/40, UN GAOR, 19th Sess., Supp. No. 40 (December 19, 2011).

[18] Christiana Ochoa, "The Relationship of Participatory Democracy to Participatory Law Formation," *Indiana Journal of Global Legal Studies* 15, no. 1 (2008), 5-18.

[19] Neil Stammers, *Human Rights and Social Movements* (New York: Pluto Press, 2009) ("the significance of the link between human rights and social movements remains largely unexplored in the specialist academic literature on human rights").

[20] Balakrishnan Rajagopal, *International Law from Below: Development, Social Movements and Third World Resistance* (Cambridge:

Cambridge University Press, 2003), 167.

[21] Ibid, 166.

[22] Julian Ku and John Yoo, "Globalization and Sovereignty," *Berkeley Journal of International Law* 31 (2013), 210, 222 (distinguishing between Westphalian sovereignty and popular sovereignty and noting, "Traditional international law reflects, in many ways the basic assumptions of the Westphalian system").

[23] Schooner Exchange v. McFaddon, 11 U.S. 116, 136 (1812).

[24] "Statute of the International Court of Justice" Article 38 (4). "Publicist" is an older term that means scholar, jurist, or commentator.

[25] Mahatma Gandhi, *Collected Works of Mahatma Gandhi,* Vol. 5 (1961), 8.

[26] Gene Sharp, *The Politics of Nonviolent Action, Vol. I: Power and Struggle* (Boston: Porter Sargent Publisher, 1973), 7–10.

[27] "Pillars of support" is a term of art in the civil resistance studies literature referring to the formal institutions and informal associations of people loyal to the regime. Pillars of support include at least six facets, including legitimacy, coercive means, control over material resources, human resources that provide the regime with technical and intelligence capabilities, and intangible factors such as culture and ideology. Gene Sharp, *The Politics of Nonviolent Action* Vol. I, 7–10.

[28] Srdja Popovic et al., *Blueprint for Revolution: How to Use Rice Pudding, Lego Men, and Other Nonviolent Techniques to Galvanize Communities, Overthrow Dictators, or Simply Change the World* (Carnegie Council, 2015), https://www.carnegiecouncil.org/en_US/studio/multimedia/20150422/index.html.

[29] Jaye Ellis, "General Principles and Comparative Law," *European Journal of International Law* 22 (2011), 952 ("regarding human rights norms, the legal fiction that states not individuals are the relevant subjects is becoming increasingly tenuous").

[30] See infra, 25.

[31] "From the standpoint of International Law and of the Court which is its organ, municipal laws are merely facts which express the will and constitute the activities of States, in the same manner as do legal decisions or administrative measures." Certain German Interests in Polish Upper Silesia (Germany v. Poland), (Merits), Permanent Court of International Justice, ser. A, No.7 (1926), 19.

[32] Bin Cheng, *General Principles of Law as Applied by International Courts and Tribunals* (Cambridge: Grotius Publications, 1987 [1953]), xv.

[33] Michelle Biddulph and Dwight Newman, "A Contextualized Account of General Principles of International Law," *Pace International Law Review* 26 (2014), 291-92.

[34] For example, in its first decision, the ICJ rested its decision on "certain general and well-recognized principles, namely: elementary considerations of humanity" rather than on treaties governing the laws of war but provided little exposition as to what these principles actually consisted of. Corfu Channel Case (United Kingdom v. Albania), 1949 ICJ 4 (April 9).

[35] Bruno Simma and Philip Alston, "The Sources of Human Rights Law: Custom, *Jus Cogens*, and General Principles," *Australian Year Book of International Law* 12 (1988-89), 107.

[36] Ibid, 108.

[37] William Blackstone, *Commentaries on the Laws of England* 4 (1765), 66, quoted in Jordan J. Paust, "Non-State Actor Participation in International Law and the Pretense of Exclusion." *Virginia Journal of International Law* 51 (2011), 998.

[38] Ware v. Hylton, 3 U.S. (3 Dall.) 199, 227 (1796) (Chase, J.).

[39] Sophocles, *Antigone* (Trans. R.C. Jebb), http://classics.mit.edu/Sophocles/antigone.html.

[40] Robert M. Cover, "The Supreme Court 1982 Term Forward: Nomos and Narrative," *Harvard Law Review*, 97 (4), 1983, 4. Cover's approach is congruent with philosophers like Charles Taylor and Cornelius Castoriadis, who theorize institutions and other social phenomena as creations of a "social imaginary."

[41] Cover himself used the term "*nomos*" to describe the result of "jurisgenesis," but Franklin G. Snyder suggests "normative universe" as a clearer alternative. Franklin G. Snyder, "Nomos, Narrative, and Adjudication: Toward a Jurisgenetic Theory of Law," *William and Mary Law Review* 40 (1999), 1624.

[42] Cover, "Nomos and Narrative," 11.

[43] Ibid, 4.

[44] Jenny S. Martinez, "Human Rights and History," *Harvard Law Review Forum* 126 (May 20, 2013), 221.

[45] These principles are in one sense descriptive. But they also are normative, in that they reflect a critical analysis of the current human rights movement and are designed to prompt the writing of movement-centered histories to guide the movement in a better direction. Of the four principles, nonviolence is the most normatively innovative, and this monograph makes an argument on its behalf. For more on the four principles, see Elizabeth A. Wilson, Be the Change: Gandhi and Human Rights (forthcoming from Columbia University Press).

[46] This critique is also sometimes made by First World scholars striving for a truly multicultural human rights perspective.

[47] Balakrishnan Rajagopal, "Culture, Resistance, and the Problems of Translating Human Rights," *Texas International Law Journal* 41 (2006), 419.

[48] Boaventura de Sousa Santos and César Rodríguez-Garavito, eds., *Law and Globalization from Below: Towards a Cosmopolitan Legality*. Cambridge Studies in Law and Society (New York: Cambridge University Press, 2005), 10.

[49] Balakrishnan Rajagopal, "The International Human Rights Movement Today," *Maryland Journal of International Law* 24 (2009), 56.

[50] Ibid.

[51] Simma and Alston, "The Sources of Human Rights Law," 85-86.

[52] Samuel Moyn, *The Last Utopia* (New York: Columbia University Press, 2010).

[53] South West Africa (Eth. v S. Afr.; Lib. v S. Afr.) Judgment, 1966 ICJ 6 (July 18) (Dissenting Opinion of Judge Tanaka), http://www. icj-cij.org/docket/files/47/4969.pdf.

[54] Anthony D'Amato, "Human Rights as Part of Customary International Law: A Plea for Change of Paradigms," *Georgia Journal of International and Comparative Law* 25 (1996), 64 ("on the level of strict logic, the idea of human rights is incompatible with the Sovereignty Paradigm [of international law]. Human rights are universal rights; they are rights against every nation in the world including one's own nation").

[55] Cicero, "Natural Law and Just War," in *War and Christian Ethics: Classic and Contemporary Readings on the Morality of War* 2nd ed. (Arthur F. Holmes, ed.) (Grand Rapids: BakerAcademic, 2005), 24.

[56] Lynn Hunt, *Inventing Human Rights* (New York: W.W. Norton & Co., 2007), 21-22.

[57] Martti Kostkienemi, *The Gentle Civilizer of Nations* (United Kingdom: Cambridge University Press, 2002), 7.

[58] Hans Kelsen, *The Law of the United Nations: A Critical Analysis of its Fundamental Problems* (New York: Frederick A. Praeger, 1950), 40.

[59] Ibid, 41.

[60] Legal scholar Bin Cheng is regarded as the first scholar to have theorized the notion of instant custom. See Bin Cheng, "Custom: The Future of General State Practice In a Divided World," in *The Structure and Process of International Law: Essays in Legal Philosophy Doctrine and Theory* 532 (R. St. J. Macdonald and Douglas M. Johnston eds.) (The Hague: Martinos Nijhoff, 1983) ("As international law is a horizontal legal system in which states are both the law-makers and the subjects of the legal system, *opinio juris* can arise or change instantaneously"); Bin Cheng, "United Nations Resolutions on Outer Space: 'Instant' International Customary Law?", *Indiana International Law Journal* 5 (1964), 23-112, repeated in *International Law: Teaching and Practice* 237, 249 (Bin Cheng ed.) (London: Stevens, 1982); see also Anthea Elizabeth Roberts, "Traditional and Modern Approaches to Customary International Law: A Reconciliation," *American Journal of International Law* 95 (2001), 758; Isabelle Gunning, "Modernizing Customary International Law: The Challenge of Human Rights," *Virginia Journal International Law* 31 (1990-91), 211; Benjamin Langille, "It's 'Instant Custom': How the Bush Doctrine Became Law After the Terrorist Attacks of September 11, 2001," *Boston College International & Comparative Law Review* 26 (2003), 156 (arguing that "[i]nstant custom, unlike traditional, slow-forming customary international law, is attuned to the rate of development in today's rapidly changing global society").

[61] Roberts, "Traditional and Modern Approaches," 758. Classic statements of customary international law are found in domestic legal cases like The Paquete Habana, 175 U.S. 677, 686 (1900) and decisions by the Permanent Court of International Justice like the S.S. "Lotus," 1927 PCIJ (ser. A) No. 10, at 18, 29 and the S.S. Wimbledon, 1923 PCIJ (ser. A) No. 1, at 25 (August 17).

[62] Roberts, "Traditional and Modern Approaches," 758; see also Thomas Meron, *Human Rights and Humanitarian Norms as Customary Law* (Oxford: Clarendon Press, 1989), 99 (referring to the "continuing process [of evolving human rights], in which *opinio juris* appears to have greater weight than state practice").

[63] In the Barcelona Traction case, the ICJ stated, "[A]n essential distinction should be drawn between the obligations of a State towards the international community as a whole, and those arising vis-à-vis another State in the field of diplomatic protection. By their very nature the former are the concern of all States. In view of the importance of the rights involved, all States can be held to have a legal interest in their protection; they are obligations *erga omnes*." Barcelona Traction, Light and Power Co. Ltd. (Belg. v. Spain), 1970 ICJ 3, 32 (February 5).

[64] Oscar Schachter, "International Law in Theory and Practice: General Course in Public International Law," *Recueil des Cours* 178, no. 21 (1982), 334-335.

[65] "Vienna Convention on the Law of Treaties" Art. 53 (1969) (defining *jus cogens* as "a norm accepted and recognized by the international community of States as a whole as a norm from which no derogation is permitted and which can be modified only by a subsequent norm of general international law having the same character"); Kamrul Hossain, "The Concept of *Jus Cogens* and the Obligation Under the UN Charter," *Santa Clara Journal of International Law* 3 (2005), (discussing *jus cogens* as a "wholly new source of law capable of generally binding rules" developed during the Vienna Conference on the Law of Treaties).

66 Anthony D'Amato, "It's a Bird, It's a Plane, It's Jus Cogens," *Connecticut Journal of International Law* 6, no. 1 (1990), 1 ("Indeed, the sheer ephemerality of *jus cogens* is an asset, enabling any writer to christen any ordinary norm of his or her choice as a new *jus cogens* norm, thereby in one stroke investing it with magical power").

67 Committee on the Formation of Customary International Law, American Branch of the International Law Association Report, "The Role of State Practice in the Formation of Customary and *Jus Cogens* Norms of International Law" (January 19, 1989), 15.

68 Louis Henkin, "Sibley Lecture, March 1994, Human Rights and State 'Sovereignty,'" *Georgia Journal of International and Comparative Law* 25 (1995-96), 38.

69 Responding to Henkin's lecture, former student Anthony D'Amato forcefully challenged him on this point. Noting that Henkin considers "outlawry of apartheid, of genocide, of slavery, of extra-judicial killing or disappearances, and of torture or inhuman treatment" as the most "basic rights," D'Amato asserted that "a majority of [national constitutions in the world] do not provide for these (or other) human rights." Anthony D'Amato, "Human Rights as Part of Customary International Law," 53. It is difficult to understand D'Amato on this point, because the evidence seems to contradict him. One hundred and thirty-two of 193 national constitutions do prohibit slavery or forced labor. One hundred and fifty-four prohibit torture. One hundred and fifty protect the right to life. One hundred and thirty-five provide for a right to health care. Even more confusing is the way he casts his alternative theory of how customary law is formed—from treaties!—as escaping the "Sovereignty Paradigm" in which he accuses Henkin of being imprisoned.

70 Anthony D'Amato, "New Approaches to Customary Law," *American Journal of International Law* 105 (2011), 163.

71 Simma and Alston, "The Sources of Human Rights Law," 88-89 and 102 (expressing concern that modern attempts to "update" customary law in the context of international protection of human rights "extend[ ] the scope of international law beyond hitherto accepted 'natural' boundaries"); see also G.J.H. Van Hoof, *Rethinking the Sources of International Law*, 86 (1983) ("[C]ustomary law and instantaneousness are irreconcilable concepts"); Anthea Elizabeth Roberts, "Traditional and Modern Approaches," 757.

72 Arthur M. Weisburd, "Customary International Law: The Problem of Treaties," *Vanderbilt Journal of Transnational Law* 21 (1988), 9 (arguing that treaty law only goes beyond declaration and becomes customary international law when "states acknowledge, at least in principle, a duty to make reparation for its breach.")

73 Hari M. Osofsky, "Climate Change Litigation As Pluralist Legal Dialogue?", *Stanford Journal of International Law* 43 (2007), 185 (rejecting the notion that international climate change litigation changes international law into a "hybrid" where "informal and subnational action could actually 'count'" because "as a practical matter, the international legal community has enough difficulties even agreeing upon what traditional international law is").

74 Anthony T. Guzman, "Saving Customary International Law," *Michigan Journal of International Law* 115 (2005), 124 (noting "it appears that *opinio juris* is necessary for there to be a rule of law, and a rule of law is necessary for there to be *opinio juris*."

75 Some commentators take a liberal view and recognize not only acts but also "diplomatic correspondence, treaties, public statements by heads of state, domestic laws." Ibid, 125. In the 1970s, the U.S. State Department stated that "government acts, including treaties, executive agreements, federal regulations, federal court decisions, and internal memoranda, were evidence of state practice but resolutions of international bodies were not." Ibid, 126. In contrast, many legal scholars "allow drafts of the International Law Commission, resolutions of the UN General Assembly, and recitals in international instruments to count as evidence of state practice. The International Law Commission itself considers the cumulative practices of international organizations as evidence of state practice." Ibid.

76 David P. Fidler, "Challenging the Classical Concept of Custom," *German Year Book of International Law* 39 (1996), 241.

77 Steve Charnovitz, "Two Centuries of Participation: NGOs and International Governance," *Michigan Journal of International Law* 18 (1997), 271. Charnovitz borrows the analytical "decision" categories from the New Haven School. See Myres S. McDougal, Harold D. Lasswell, and W. Michael Reisman, eds., "The World Constitutive Process of Authoritative Decision," in *International Law Essays: A Supplement to International Law in Contemporary Perspective* (1981), 219, 221-22, 267-69.

78 The UN Charter provides for discretionary consultation in Art. 71 ("The Economic and Social Council may make suitable arrangements for consultation with nongovernmental organizations which are concerned with matters within its competence..."). "The Charter of the United Nations" (1945), Article 71. The Economic and Social Council Resolution regulating the ECOSOC's relation with CSOs also makes clear that the relationship is discretionary. Consultative relationship between the United Nations and nongovernmental organizations, Economic and Social Council, 49th plenary meeting (United Nations, 1996), paragraph 5 ("Consultative relationships may be established with international, regional, sub-regional and national organizations, in conformity with the Charter of the United Nations and the principles and criteria established under the present resolution.")

79 Charnovitz, "Two Centuries of Participation," 272.

80 Janet Koven Levitt, "A Bottom-Up Approach to International Lawmaking: The Tale of Three Trade Finance Instruments," *Yale*

Journal of International Law 30 (2005), 128.

[81] Stanley Hoffmann et al., "Mild Reformist and Mild Revolutionary," *Journal of International Affairs* 24 (1970), 120.

[82] Jordan J. Paust, "Non-State Actor Participation in International Law and the Pretense of Exclusion," *Virginia Journal of International Law* 51 (2011), 1001.

[83] Ibid, 994.

[84] Ibid, 1000.

[85] Elizabeth A. Wilson, "'People Power' and the Problem of Sovereignty in International Law," *Duke Journal of Comparative and International Law* 26 (2016), 581-586.

[86] Margaret E. Keck and Kathryn Sikkink, *Activists Beyond Borders: Advocacy Networks in International Politics* (Ithaca: Cornell University Press, 1998).

[87] Marlies Glasius, *The International Criminal Court: A GCS Achievement* (London: Routledge, 2005).

[88] Charnovitz, "Two Centuries of Participation," 183-286; Steve Charnovitz, "Nongovernmental Organizations and International Law," *American Journal of International Law* 100 (2006), 348-372.

[89] Gunning, "Modernizing Customary International Law," 213.

[90] Julie Mertus, "Considering Nonstate Actors in the New Millennium: Toward Expanded Participation in Norm Generation and Norm Application," *New York University Journal of International Law and Policy* 32 (2000), 561.

[91] Peter J. Spiro, "New Global Potentates: Nongovernmental Organizations and the 'Unregulated' Marketplace," *Cardozo Law Review* 18 (1996), 959-60.

[92] Till Müller, "Customary Transnational Law: Attacking the Last Resort of State Sovereignty," *Indiana Journal of Global Legal Studies* 15 (2008), 27.

[93] Ochoa, "The Individual and Customary International Law Formation," *Virginia Journal of International Law* 48 (2007), passim.

[94] Ibid, 164-68.

[95] Ibid, 124.

[96] Ibid, 121, 178-83 ("The role of non-state actors in the formation of CIL has not been adequately considered or explored"). Of the four types of evidence she considers, three are arguably mediated by elites. General Assembly Resolutions are made by states, not individuals. NGOs are self-selected and not necessarily representative of the people as a whole. Human rights litigation is undertaken by elites on behalf of others and is shaped by a host of considerations other than the subjective beliefs and expectations of the people regarding their rights.

[97] Myres S. McDougal, Harold D. Lasswell, and W. Michael Reisman, "Theories About International Law: Prologue to a Configurative Jurisprudence," *Virginia Journal of International Law* 8 (1968), 193.

[98] McDougal, Lasswell, and Reisman summarize these functions as follows: "1. Intelligence is the obtaining, processing, and dissemination of information (including planning); 2. Promotion (or recommendation) is the advocacy of general policy; 3. Prescription is the crystallization of general policy in continuing authoritative community expectations; 4. Invocation is the provisional characterization of concrete circumstances in reference to prescriptions; 5. Application is the final characterization of concrete circumstances according to prescriptions. 6. Termination is the ending of a prescription and the disposition of legitimate expectations created when the prescription was in effect; 7. Appraisal is the evaluation of the manner and measure in which public policies have been put into effect and of responsibility therefor." Ibid, 192.

[99] Ibid, 192-93 ("While the public functions of prescription and application are necessarily restricted, in terms of direct participation, participation in all other functions presents almost unlimited democratic potential.")

[100] Hengameh Saberi, "Love It or Hate It, but for the Right Reasons: Pragmatism and the New Haven School's International Law of Human Dignity," *Boston College International & Comparative Law Review* 35 (2012), 59.

[101] Stanley Anderson, "A Critique of Professor Myres S. McDougal's Doctrine of Interpretation by Major Purposes," *American Journal of International Law* 57 (1963), 382.

[102] Ochoa, "Individual and Customary International Law Formation," 176.

[103] See Niels Petersen, "Customary Law Without Custom? Rules, Principles, and the Role of State Practice in International Norm Creation," *American University International Law Review* 23 (2008), 277 (arguing "that certain categories of legal norms should be classified as general principles of international law instead of custom, and thus should not require the proof of state practice as a constituent element.")

[104] Bin Cheng, *General Principles of Law as Applied by International Courts and Tribunals* (Cambridge: Grotius Publications, 1987 [1953]), xv (describing general principles as "the most controversial of the various sources of international law enumerated in Article 38 of the Statute and thus of international law in general"); Neha Jain, "Judicial Lawmaking and General Principles of Law in

International Criminal Law," *Harvard International Law Journal*, 57, no. 1 (Winter 2016), 112, 125 (describing general principles as "[o]ne of the most flexible, but deeply controversial, sources in [the] arsenal" of judges in international criminal courts," with a "mysterious and perplexing nature"); Elena Carpanelli, "General Principles of International Law: Struggling with a Slippery Concept," *Ius Gentium* 46 (2015), 125 ("The methodology and evidence needed for inducing them from municipal law is controversial"); Ellis, "General Principles and Comparative Law," 949 (calling general principles "highly controversial and largely neglected").

[105] Carpanelli, "General Principles of International Law," 125-26.

[106] Ellis, "General Principles and Comparative Law," 954 (identifying the consensus as involving "first, the identification of a principle that is common to municipal legal orders belonging to the main legal systems of the world; secondly, the distillation of the essence of the principle. To these is often added a third, namely modifying the principle to suit the particularities of international law.")

[107] Ibid, 949.

[108] Biddulph and Newman, "A Contextualized Account of General Principles," 290.

[109] Biddulph and Newman point out a difference between majority and separate and dissenting opinions in terms of terminological and methodological clarity.

[110] Henkin (quoted in Simma and Alston 108) (referring to general principles as "this secondary source"); M. G. Danilenko, *Law-Making in the International Community* (1993), 186 (asserting general principles "at best would appear to retain only the status of a subsidiary source of law"). D'Amato, "Human Rights as Part of Customary International Law," 51-52 ("The generally accepted view of international scholars is that there are only two sources of international law: customary and conventional.")

[111] Judge Simma's separate opinion in the Oil Platforms case is an example of this comparatist approach. Oil Platforms (Iran v. U.S.), Judgment, 2003 ICJ. 324, P66 (November 6) (separate opinion of Judge Simma), http://www.icj-cij.org/docket/files/9C/9735.pdf (concluding on the basis of "modest" comparative survey that joint and several liability is a general principle of law); see also Jaye Ellis, "General Principles and Comparative Law," *European Journal of International Law* 22 (2011), 949.

[112] Tyler G. Banks, "Corporate Liability Under the Alien Tort Statute: The Second Circuit's Misstep Around General Principles of Law in Kiobel v. Royal Dutch Petroleum Co.," *Emory International Law Review* 26 (2012), 247-48.

[113] Biddulph and Newman, "A Contextualized Account of General Principles," 286 (noting "There has been little development of methodology under this approach"); Thomas M. Franck, "Non-Treaty Law-Making: When, Where, and How?," in *Developments of International Law in Treaty Making* (Rüdger Wolfrum and Volker Röben eds.) (2005), 423.

[114] Simma and Alston, "The Sources of Human Rights Law," 102.

[115] See, e.g., Oscar Schachter, "International Law in Theory and Practice," *Developments in International Law* 13 (M. Nijhoff, 1991), 54–55 (describing general principles as including universalist principle that are "valid through all kinds of human societies"); South West Africa (Eth. v. S. Afr.; Lib. v. S. Afr.) Judgment, 1966 ICJ. 6 (July 18) (dissenting opinion of Judge Tanaka) ("As an interpretation of Article 38, paragraph 1 (c), we consider that the concept of human rights and of their protection is included in the general principles mentioned in that Article"), http://www.icj-cij.org/docket/files/47/4969.pdf.

[116] Louis Henkin, "International Law: Politics, Values and Functions: General Course in Public International Law," 216 *Recueil des cours* (1989-IV), 61-62.

[117] Schachter, *International Law in Theory and Practice*, 50–53; Gerald G. Fitzmaurice, "The General Principles of International Law considered from the Standpoint of the Rule of Law," in *Collected Courses of the Hague Academy of International Law* 92 (Brill: Boston, 1957); Mavrommatis Palestinian Concessions (Greece v. Brit.), 1924. PCIJ. (ser. A) No. 2, at 12 (August 30).

[118] Sidney L. Harring, "German Reparations to the Herero Nation: An Assertion of Herero Nationhood in the Path of Namibian Development?," *West Virginia Law Review* 104 (2002), 407 (describing Jewish and Japanese reparations claims as not based on the Hague Convention "but on more general principles of human rights"); Jon L. Jacobson, "At-Sea Interception of Alien Migrants: International Law Issues," *Willamette Law Review* 28 (1992), 818 (noting that the U.S. policy of interdicting migrants at sea is "inconsistent with general principles of human rights law and morally unacceptable" even if "technically legal").

[119] See, e.g., Alexander P. Sario, "Return to Sender: Reconsidering Prisoner Correspondence Under Article 8 in Dankevich v. Ukraine," *Loyola of Los Angeles International & Comparative Law Review* 28 (2006), 199 (referring to "general principles of human rights articulated in the UDHR); Kavitha R. Giridhar, "Justice for All: Protecting the Translation Rights of Defendants in International War Crime Tribunals," *Case Western Reserve Journal of International Law* 43 (2011), 801 (noting the "UDHR sets forth general principles of human rights").

[120] M. Cherif Bassiouni, "Human Rights in the Context of Criminal Justice: Identifying International Procedural Protections and Equivalent Protections in National Constitutions," *Duke Journal of Comparative and International Law* 3 (1993), 239.

[121] Simma and Alston, "The Sources of Human Rights Law," 102.

[122] Ibid.

123 Such work might even be a model for developing searchable datasets on state practice to help simplify the process of determining customary international law. The International Committee for the Red Cross created a database for humanitarian law and the laws of war, but it has been justifiably criticized for not being focused enough on state practice.

124 Bidculph and Newman, "A Contextualized Account of General Principles," 301.

125 The Nonviolent and Violent Campaigns and Outcomes dataset (NAVCO 1.0) was first introduced in Erica Chenoweth and Maria J. Stephan, "Why Civil Resistance Works," 9-10. The version of the dataset used for the 2011 book (NAVCO 1.1) was published as an online appendix. Erica Chenoweth, NAVCO Dataset, v. 1.1, University of Denver, available for download at http://www.du.edu/korbel/sie/research/chenow_navco_data.html.

126 Jonathan Pinckney, *Making and Breaking Nonviolent Discipline in Civil Resistance Movements*, ICNC Monograph Series, 2016. https://www.nonviolent-conflict.org/making-or-breaking-nonviolent-discipline-in-civil-resistance-movements/.

127 Henkin, "Sibley Lecture," 39.

128 Ibid, 40.

129 Hurst Hannum, "The Status of the Universal Declaration of Human Rights in National and International Law," *Georgia Journal of International and Comparative Law* 25 (1995/96), 312.

130 Nihal Jayawickrama, "Hong Kong and the International Protection of Human Rights," in *Human Rights in Hong Kong* (Raymond Wicks ed.) (Hong Kong: Oxford University Press, 1992), 160, no. 99. According to Hannum, "Many African constitutions in the immediate post-independence period made explicit reference to the UDHR, including those of Algeria (1963), Burundi (1962), Cameroon (1960), Chad (1960), Democratic Republic of the Congo (later Zaïre) (1964 and 1967), Republic of the Congo (1963), Dahomey (1964 and 1968), Equatorial Guinea (1968), Gabon (1961), Guinea (1958), Ivory Coast (1960), Madagascar (1959), Mali (1960), Mauritania (1962), Niger (1960), Rwanda (1962), Senegal (1963), Somalia (1979), Togo (1963), and Upper Volta (now Burkina Faso) (1960 and 1970)." Hannum, "Status of the Universal Declaration," 313 (citing United Nations, *United Nations Actions in the Field of Human Rights* (New York: United Nations, 1974), 17. "Among constitutions currently in force, the Declaration is specifically referred to in those of Afghanistan, Benin, Burkina Faso, Burundi, Cambodia, Chad, Comoros, Côte d'Ivoire, Equatorial Guinea, Ethiopia 1991 Transitional Charter), Gabon, Guinea, Haiti, Malawi, Mali, Mauritania, Nicaragua, Niger, Portugal, Romania, Rwanda, Sao Tomé and Principe, Senegal, Somalia, Spain, and Togo"). Ibid, 313.

131 Harold Hongju Koh, "Why Do Nations Obey International Law?," *Yale Law Journal* 106 (1997), 2599-2659, 2657 (noting that "[f]or activists, the constructive role of international law in the post-Cold War era will be greatly enhanced if nongovernmental organizations seek self-consciously to participate in, influence, and ultimately enforce transnational legal process by promoting the internalization of international norms into domestic law.")

132 Ibid.

133 These figures have been compiled by Jordanian freedom of information expert and journalist, Yahia Shukkeir.

134 HRC, General Comment 34, U.N. Doc. CCPR/C/GC/34 at para. 19: "To give effect to the right of access to information, States parties should proactively put in the public domain Government information of public interest… States parties should also enact the necessary procedures, whereby one may gain access to information, such as by means of freedom of information legislation."

135 The post-war Japanese Constitution, in Article 97, described the "fundamental human rights" guaranteed by the Constitution as the "fruits of the age-old struggle of man to be free; they have survived the many exacting tests for durability."

136 *An Account of the Proceedings on the Trial of Susan B. Anthony on the Charge of Illegal Voting at the Presidential Election in November, 1872, and on the Trial of Beverly W. Jones, Edwin T. Marsh and William B. Hall, the Inspectors of Elections by Whom Her Vote Was Received* (Rochester: Daily Democrat and Chronicle Book Print, 1874), 151–78. http://www.fjc.gov/history/home.nsf/page/tu_anthony_doc_13.html.

137 *Maidan*, directed by Sergei Loznitsa (Netherlands: Atoms and Void, 2014).

138 Ibid (one speaker says, "we do not recognize their laws.")

139 Greg Michener, "FOI Laws Around the World," *Journal of Democracy* 22, no. 2 (April 2011), 155.

140 Ibid.

141 Ibid.

142 Aruna Roy and Nikhil Dey, "The Right to Information: Facilitating People's Participation and State Accountability," 4.

143 Ibid.

144 Greg Michener, "FOI Laws Around the World," *Journal of Democracy* 22, no. 2 (April 2011), 155.

145 Ibid, 156.

146 Ibid.

147 "Freedom of Information Laws Around the World," WNYC: On the Media (November 18, 2011), http://www.wnyc.org/story/171307-

freedom-information-laws-around-world/#commentlist.

148 Fitzmaurice, "General Principles," 7.

149 For a fuller argument, see Wilson, Be the Change (forthcoming).

150 These principles are in one sense descriptive. But they also are normative, in that they reflect a critical analysis of the current human rights movement and are designed to prompt the writing of movement-centered histories to guide the movement in a better direction. Of the four principles, nonviolence is the most normatively innovative, and this monograph makes an argument on its behalf.

151 Rex D. Glensy, "The Right to Dignity," *Columbia Human Rights Law Review* 43 (2011), 104.

152 UDHR, Preamble, GA Res. 217A (III), U.N. Doc. A/810 (1948) (affirming "faith in fundamental human rights" that include, among others, "the dignity and worth of the human person.")

153 Article 1 ("All human beings are born free and equal in dignity and rights. They are endowed with reason and conscience and should act towards one another in a spirit of brotherhood"); Article 22 ("Everyone ... has the right to social security and is entitled to realization ... of the economic, social and cultural rights indispensable for his dignity and the free development of his personality"; and Article 23 ("Everyone who works has the right to just and favorable remuneration ensuring for himself and his family an existence worthy of human dignity.")

154 Maciej Bartkowski and Annyssa Bellal, "A Human Right to Resist," openDemocracy (May 3, 2011), https://www.opendemocracy.net/maciej-bartkowski-annyssa-bellal/human-right-to-resist.

155 Ibid.

156 Quoted in Arista M. Cirtautis, *The Polish Solidarity Movement: Revolution, Democracy, and Natural Rights* (Taylor & Francis, 2002), 168.

157 Larbi Sidiki, "Tunisia: Portrait One of a Revolution," *Al Jazeera* (January 15, 2012), http://www.aljazeera.com/indepth/opinion/2012/01/2012114121925380575.html.

158 Interview, David Ottoway.

159 Quoted in Bartkowski and Bellal, "Human Right to Resist."

160 Ibid.

161 Anne Barnard, "Lebanese Protesters Aim for Rare Unity Against Gridlocked Government," *The New York Times*, August 29, 2015, http://www.nytimes.com/2015/08/30/world/middleeast/lebanon-protests-garbage-government-corruption.html.

162 Jeff Abbott, "Guatemala: Popular Protests Challenge Corruption and the Political Establishment," (May 18, 2015), www.upsidedownworld.org.

163 M'du Hlongwa, XinWei Ngiam, "Taking Poverty Seriously: What the Poor are Saying and Why it Matters," (2006), https://abahlali.org/node/27/.

164 Quoted in Cirtautas, *The Polish Solidarity Movement*, 174.

165 Abahlali baseMjondolo statement to The Human Rights Commission, *The Occupied Times* (March 9, 2015), https://theoccupiedtimes.org/?p=13714

A representative from Abahlali baseMjondolo addressing the South African Human Rights Commission said, "When we say that we are struggling for dignity we mean that we are struggling for a society in which each person is recognised as a human being. This means that they must be treated with respect but also that they must have access to all that a person needs for a dignified life – land, housing, education, a livelihood and so on." Statement for the Human Rights Commission Hearings Relating to Access to Housing, Local Government and Service Delivery.

166 Rebecca Burns, "South Africa's Rebellion of the Poor," Waging Nonviolence (November 5, 2010), http://wagingnonviolence.org/feature/south-africas-rebellion-of-the-poor/.

167 United States Library of Congress, "Today in History: 8-Hour Work Day", https://www.loc.gov/item/today-in-history/august-20.

168 International Bill of Rights refers to the Universal Declaration of Human Rights (1948), the International Covenant on Economic, Social and Cultural Rights (1966), and the International Covenant on Civil and Political Rights and its two Optional Protocols (1966).

169 Likewise, Article 12 provides: 1) "Everyone has the right, individually and in association with others, to participate in peaceful activities against violations of human rights and fundamental freedoms. 3)...everyone is entitled, individually and in association with others, to be protected effectively under national law in reacting against or opposing, through peaceful means, activities and acts, including those by omission, attributable to States that result in violations of human rights and fundamental freedoms, as well as acts of violence perpetrated by groups or individuals that affect the enjoyment of human rights and fundamental freedoms. Article 13 ensures the right to resources "for the express purpose of promoting and protecting human rights and fundamental freedoms through peaceful means... "

170 "Who is a Defender?," UN Human Rights Office of the High Commissioner, http://www.ohchr.org/EN/Issues/SRHRDefenders/

Pages/Defender.aspx.

[171] For a discussion of how even strategic nonviolence has ineluctable moral dimensions, see Chaiwat Satha-Anand, "Overcoming Illusory Division: Between Nonviolence as a Pragmatic Strategy and a Principled Way of Life," in Kurt Schock ed., *Civil Resistance: Comparative Perspectives on Nonviolent Struggle* (Minneapolis: University of Minnesota Press, 2015).

[172] "Study: Nonviolent Civic Resistance Key Factor in Building Durable Democracies," Freedom House (May 24, 2005), https://freedomhouse.org/article/study-nonviolent-civic-resistance-key-factor-building-durable-democracies.

[173] Ibid.

[174] Patrick M. Regan, "Third-party Interventions and the Duration of Intrastate Conflicts," *Journal of Conflict Resolution* 46, no. 1 (2002), 71

[175] Chenoweth and Stephan, *Why Civil Resistance Works.*

[176] Ibid, 217.

[177] Col. Robert Helvey, *On Strategic Nonviolent Conflict: Thinking About the Fundamentals* (Boston: The Albert Einstein Institution, 2004), xi.

[178] Brian Martin, *Justice Ignited: The Dynamics of Backfire* (Lanham: Rowman & Littlefield, 2007).

[179] Perhaps because it is less obvious how the social and economic rights of participants are relevant to civil resistance movements, the discussion about the components of the right to peaceful protest tends to focus on civil and political rights. But it should be noted that, depending on state ratifications, the ICESCR as well protects participants in nonviolent civil resistance movements. Social and economic rights could be implicated in certain situations, such as if during large-scale encampments in public spaces like Tahrir Square, the government responded by cutting off public water supplies or prevented supporters from bringing in food and materials for shelter. Cultural rights could be implicated if the protests are staged by minority or indigenous groups, or if they involve cultural heritage sites.

[180] The language of the limitations varies slightly with respect to the different rights. Most require that the limitations be imposed through lawful measures and are only such as are "necessary" to achieve the public purpose at issue.

[181] As of August 2016, of 1007 total Views adopted by the Human Rights Committee, only 20 involved, even in part, Article 22 (right to association) and only 33 involved Article 21 (right to peaceful assembly). Of the 33 Views dealing with peaceful assembly, 26 were from Belarus.

[182] Pursuant to Art. 4 of the ICCPR, a state can lawfully derogate from (i.e., violate) its obligations "[i]n time of public emergency which threatens the life of the nation and the existence of which is officially proclaimed." ICCPR, Art. 4(1). "No derogation from articles 6, 7, 8 (paragraphs I and 2), 11, 15, 16 and 18 may be made under this provision." Art. 4(2).

[183] "Seminar on effective measures and best practices to ensure the promotion and protection of human rights in the context of peaceful protests," UNHRC, Twenty-fifth Session (UNGA, 2014).

[184] "The promotion and protection of human rights in the context of peaceful protests," UNHRC, Twenty-fifth Session (UNGA, 2014), para. 3.

[185] Stankov v. Bulgaria (App 29221/95 and 29225/95) ECtHR judgment October 2, 2001.

[186] UNHRC, "Promotion and protection of human rights," para. 20.

[187] Perhaps because the intended audience is member states of the United Nations, the Joint Report refers only twice to "peaceful protest," but one reference is to the language on peaceful protest in UNHRC Res. 25/38, that the special rapporteurs said especially guided them to focus on assemblies that "express a common position, grievance, aspiration or identity and that diverge from mainstream positions or challenge established political, social, cultural or economic interests" (para. 11).

[188] The Joint Report defines "assembly" as "an intentional and temporary gathering in a private or public space for a specific purpose, and can take the form of demonstrations, meetings, strikes, processions, rallies or sit-ins with the purpose of voicing grievances and aspirations or facilitating celebrations...." (para. 10). An assembly may include sporting events, concerts, and related gatherings, and it applies to online virtual gatherings as well.

[189] Art. 20 (providing 1. Any propaganda for war shall be prohibited by law. 2. Any advocacy of national, racial or religious hatred that constitutes incitement to discrimination, hostility or violence shall be prohibited by law).

[190] See, e.g., Gene Sharp, "198 Methods of Nonviolent Action," http://www.aeinstein.org/nonviolentaction/198-methods-of-nonviolent-action/.

[191] Rules of Procedure of the IAHRC on Human Rights, Art. 25.

[192] Ibid, Art. 25(2)(a)-(c).

[193] For example, the IAHRC received a request for precautionary measures in the case of Asunto Américo de Grazia on May 13, 2016 and issued the requested measures on July 21, 2016. Comisión Interamericana de Derechos Humanos Resolución 41/2016, http://

www.oas.org/es/cidh/decisiones/pdf/2016/MC359-16-ES.pdf.

194 Francisco J. Quintana, "Inter-American Commission Grants Precautionary Measures to Save the Life of Beatriz," O'Neill Institute Blog, http://www.oneillinstituteblog.org/inter-american-commission-grants-precautionary-measures-to-save-the-life-of-beatriz/.

195 Center for Justice and International Law and International Human Rights Law Clinic, University of California, Berkeley, School of Law, *Comparative Analysis of the Practice of Precautionary Measures Among International Human Rights Bodies Submitted to Special Meeting of the Permanent Council of the Organization of American States* (December 2012), 10 (noting "[t]he lack of a public archive of decisions on precautionary measures"); Diego Rodriguez-Pinzón, "Precautionary Measures of the Inter-American Commission on Human Rights: Legal Status and Importance," *Human Rights Brief* 20, no. 2 (Winter 2013), 16 (noting "the Commission has issued more than 780 precautionary measures from 1995 to 2012, focusing mostly on the core basic rights recognized by the human rights instruments").

196 "Views" are issued in response to individual complaints.

197 Vadzim Bylina, "Public Protests in Belarus: The Opposition is Changing Tactics" (March 12, 2014), (summarizing an untranslated report by the Institute of Political Science, "Political Sphere," *Protest Activity in Belarus in 2013: manifestations, political performance, and social conflicts*), https://belarusdigest.com/story/public-protests-in-belarus-the-opposition-is-changing-tactics/

198 Personal communication from creator of Facebook page.

199 Case of Diaz Pena v. Venezuela, Judgment (June 26, 2012) (Preliminary objection, merits, reparations and costs).

200 The decision in Pena's case followed an earlier decision against Venezuela in a case filed by opposition leader, Leopoldo Lopez Mendoza, who had been imprisoned on politically-motivated charges. Leopoldo Lopez Mendoza v. Venezuela, Case 12.668, Inter-American Commission on Human Rights, OEA/Ser.L./V/II, doc. 51 (2009).

201 Organization of American States Press Release, "IACHR Regrets Decision of Venezuela to Denounce the American Convention on Human Rights" (September 12, 2012), http://www.oas.org/en/iachr/media_center/PReleases/2012/117.asp.

202 International Service for Human Rights, "Venezuela: Human rights defenders look to United Nations for justice and accountability" (January 9, 2015), http://www.ishr.ch/news/venezuela-human-rights-defenders-look-un-justice-and-accountability-0.

203 Kevin J. O'Brien and Lianjiang Li, *Rightful Resistance in Rural China* (Cambridge: Cambridge University Press: 2000).

204 Kurt Schock, "Rightful Radical Resistance: Mass Mobilization and Land Struggles in India and Brazil," *Mobilization: An International Quarterly* 20 no. 4 (2015), 493-515.

205 Lauren Hilgers, "Hong Kong's Umbrella Revolution Isn't Over Yet," *New York Times Magazine* (February 18, 2015), http://www.nytimes.com/2015/02/22/mag-azine/hong-kongs-umbrella-revolution-isnt-over-yet.html.

206 China signed the ICCPR in 1998, but has not yet ratified it. Under international law, signing a treaty commits a state, at a minimum, to striving not to defeat the object and purpose of the treaty.

207 Joint Declaration on the Question of Hong Kong, China-U.K, December 19, 1984, 1399 U.N.T.S. 33 (coming into force in 1985). The last paragraph of Chap. XIII in Annex I provides: "The provisions of the International Covenant on Civil and Political Rights and the International Covenant on Economic, Social and Cultural Rights as applied to Hong Kong shall remain in force." Alvin Y.H. Cheung, "Road to Nowhere: Hong Kong's Democratization and China's Obligations Under Public International Law," *Brook Journal of International Law* 40 (2015), 465, 478 (2015).

208 There is a highly technical argument about whether, despite the applicability of the ICCPR, political participation rights may still lawfully be limited. Because of Hong Kong's status as a colony, Britain had entered a reservation to Article 25 of the ICCPR ("political participation rights"), the existence of which has created space for a legal argument about the extent of the treaty's application in Hong Kong. Legal scholar Cheung cites the 1995 HRC Concluding Observations where the HRC said that the reservation no longer applies. Cheung, "Road to Nowhere." However, the latest concluding observations from the HRC, published on April 29, 2013, acknowledged the reservation and the need to eliminate it (para. 6). HRC, Concluding Observations on the Third Periodic Report of Hong Kong, China, 107th Sess., March 11-28, 2013, para. 6, U.N. Doc. CCPR/C/CHN-HKG/CO/3 (April 29, 2013).

209 Ben Blanchard, "China Says U.N. Rights Covenant No Measure for Hong Kong Reform," *Reuters* (October 24, 2014), http://www.reuters.com/article/2014/10/24/us-china-hongkong-un-idUSKCN0ID14U20141024#chQqFeLDQMHdVbgm.99.

210 Michael Martina, et. al., "Chinese Foreign Ministry spokeswoman Hua Chunying acknowledged that the covenant applied to Hong Kong," *Reuters,* http://www.reuters.com/article/us-china-hongkong-un-idUSKCN0ID14U20141024.

211 Michael Caster, "Internationalizing rights-based resistance in China: the U.N. Human Rights Council and the citizen," openDemocracy, https://www.opendemocracy.net/civilresistance/michael-caster/internationalizing-rights-based-resistance-in-china-un-human-rights-c.

212 Sohair Riad, "Local Media Coverage of the UPR: Egypt and Bahrain as Case Studies" (draft paper, Cairo Institute for Human Rights Studies) (undated).

[213] Laura E. Landolt, "Externalizing Human Rights: From Commission to Council, the Universal Periodic Review, and Egypt." *Human Rights Review* 14 (2), 2013, 125.

[214] Ibid.

[215] Egypt's review session had taken place on February 17th.

[216] The Forum of Independent Human Rights Organizations, "Human Rights in Egypt in 100 Days," press conference (June 7, 2010), http://www.cihrs.org/?p=16915&lang=en.

[217] Riad, "Local Media Coverage of the UPR," 21 (citing *Al Shorouk*, Ba'ad sa'aat men hadethat al askandeya, ishada 'arabeya be taqreer masr le hoqooq al insan! (June 11, 2010)). *Al Shorouk* published another piece linking the UPR review and Saeed's death, called "The culture of emergency from Geneva to Alexandria." Ibid., 22 (citing *Al Shorouk*, Thaqafat Al Tawaree' men geneve ila al askandareya (June 17, 2010)).

[218] Ibid, 22.

[219] Ilana Landsberg-Lewis, ed., "Implementing the Convention on Eliminating All Forms of Discrimination Against Women," *Bringing Equality Home* (New York: United Nations Development Fund For Women (UNIFEM), 1998), 29.

[220] Ibid.

[221] Ibid.

[222] Rana Husseini, *Murder in the Name of Honor: The True Story of One Woman's Heroic Fight Against an Unbelievable Crime* (New York: OneWorld Publishers: 2009), 33.

[223] Ibid, 35.

[224] Final Act of the Conference on Security and Co-operation in Europe (Helsinki Final Act), art. 7, August 1, 1975, 14 I.L.M. 1292 (1975).

[225] Daniel Charles Thomas, *The Helsinki Effect: International Norms, Human Rights, and the Demise of Communism* (Princeton: Princeton University Press, 2001), 105.

[226] Ihor Gawdihok, *Czechoslovakia: A Country Study* (Washington: Library of Congress, 1989), 238.

[227] Ludmila Alexeeva, "Article by Ludmila Alexeeva," OSCE (October 13, 2010), https://www.osce.org/home/106317.

[228] Thomas, *The Helsinki Effect*, 59.

[229] Ibid, 221.

[230] David Wolman, "The Instigators," *The Atavist Magazine*, no. 4, https://read.atavist.com/the-instigators?no-overlay&promo).

[231] Ibid see also Wael Ghonim, *Revolution 2.0* (London: Fourth Estate, 2012).

[232] Lecture, Seton Hall University (November 13, 2014).

[233] Veronique Dudouet and Howard Clark, *Directorate-General for External Policies, Policy Department report, Nonviolent Civil Action in Support of Human Rights and Democracy*, (Brussels: European Parliament, 2009), 10.

[234] See Adam Roberts, "Civil Resistance and the Fate of the Arab Spring," in *Civil Resistance in the Arab Spring: Triumphs and Disasters* (eds. Adam Roberts, Michael J. Willis, Rory McCarthy, and Timothy Garton Ash) (Oxford: Oxford University Press, 2016).

[235] Vaclav Havel, "The Power of the Powerless," in *The Power of the Powerless: Citizens against the state in central-eastern Europe*, ed. John Keane (Armonk: Palach Press, 1985), 30-31.

[236] Ibid 41.

[237] Ibid 42.

[238] Ibid 60.

[239] Ibid 75.

[240] Ibid 76.

[241] Ibid, 69.

[242] Ibid

[243] Ibid 76.

[244] Ibid 27-29.

[245] Ibid 39-41.

[246] Ibid 39.

[247] SASO, "Policy Manifesto," https://www.sahistory.org.za/archive/south-african-students-organisation-saso-policy-manifesto.

[248] Sean Chabot and Stellan Vinthagen, "Decolonizing Civil Resistance," *Mobilization: An International Quarterly* 20 (4), 2015, 527-28.

[249] Olga Onuch, "EuroMaidan Protests in Ukraine: Social Media Versus Social Networks," *Problems of Post-Communism* 62 (2015), 217-235.

[250] Ibid 225.

[251] Ibid, 227.

252 Ibid, 225.

253 Ibid, 225.

254 Ibid, 217.

255 Ibid.

256 "Arab Barometer" is a scholarly research partnership between U.S. and Middle Eastern universities and research centers. Since 2006, it has conducted periodic surveys of political attitudes in the Middle East at regular intervals through a set of surveys administered to randomly selected respondents in various Middle Eastern countries. Regular surveys were scheduled to be done in Tunisia and Egypt while the Arab Spring was going on in both countries. Researchers took advantage of this by designing supplemental surveys to identify individuals who were participating in the demonstrations. Because it randomly targeted individuals in Tunisa and Egypt, only a small number of those who filled out the surveys were participating in the protests. In Egypt, ninety-eight of 1,220 people surveyed (eight percent) reported having participated in the protests, while in Tunisia, 192 of 1,196 (sixteen percent) reported participating. Beissinger, et al, "Who Participated in the Arab Spring? A Comparison of Egyptian and Tunisian Revolutions," 3. The survey was "cold" rather than "hot" like the one at Euromaidan because it was retrospective; no questions were asked of demonstrators while they were in the process of demonstrating, and no open-ended questions were asked.

257 "Codebook Arab Democracy Barometer Wave III," Arab Barometer, 2012-2014, 35, http://www.arabbarometer.org/content/arab-barometer-iii-0.

258 "I am a Ukrainian," https://www.youtube.com/watch?v=Hvds2AliWLA.

259 Revolution viva, vive la people, http://blog.jaluo.com/.

260 Sidiki, "Tunisia: Portrait One."

261 Article 21 of the UDHR provides "(3) The will of the people shall be the basis of the authority of government," but this language was not adopted in the ICCPR. Article 25 of the ICCPR is weaker: "Every citizen shall have the right and the opportunity, without any of the distinctions mentioned in article 2 and without unreasonable restrictions... (b) To vote and to be elected at genuine periodic elections which shall be by universal and equal suffrage and shall be held by secret ballot, guaranteeing the free expression of the will of the electors."

262 Interview with Jamel Betteib, July 2, 2015.

263 Makau wa Mutua, "Hope and Despair for a New South Africa: the Limits of Rights Discourse," Harvard Human Rights 10 (1997), 65. South Africa commemorates the Sharpville massacre on March 21st, as "Human Rights Day.

264 Penelope E. Andrews, "Incorporating International Human Rights Law into Domestic Constitutions: the South African Experience," in Russell A. Miller and Rebecca Bratspies, Progress in International Law (Leiden: Martinus Nijhoff Publishers, 2008).

265 The 1997 Polish Constitution also includes human rights and social justice principles and is arguably a reflection of the Solidarity movement.

266 Jean-Marie Henckaerts and Stefaan Van Der Jeught, "Human Rights Protection under the New Constitutions of Central Europe," Loyola of Los Angeles International and Comparative Law Review 20 (1998), 478. The Slovak Republic incorporated the Charter of Fundamental Rights and Freedoms directly into its constitution. Ibid. USTAVA SLOVENSKJ REPUBLIKY [Constitution] Arts. 11-54 (Slovk.), reprinted in The Rebirth of Democracy - 12 Constitutions of Central and Eastern Europe (2nd ed), (ed. International Institute of Democracy) (Strasbourg: Council of Europe Publ., 1996), 327-60.

267 Maidan, [the film].

268 Sidiki, "Tunisia: Portrait One."

269 Maidan, [the film].

270 On the nonviolent dimension of the Euromaidan revolution and its violent flank see Maciej Bartkowski and Maria Stephan, "How Ukraine Ousted an Autocrat. The Logic of Civil Resistance," Atlantic Council (June 1, 2014), http://www.atlanticcouncil.org/publications/articles/how-ukraine-ousted-an-autocrat-the-logic-of-civil-resistance.

271 Howard Barrell, lecture at the ICNC Summer Institute for the Advanced Study of Nonviolent Conflict, "A Violent Flank that Fired a Blank: Civil Resistance and Armed Insurgency in the Struggle Against Apartheid," June 2013.

272 Another example of a movement whose nonviolent commitments are unclear at this writing is found in Iraq, where a former Shiite militia has ostensibly been transformed into a nonviolent organization engaged primarily in providing social services but also in public protests. At the time of the US invasion of Iraq, powerful cleric Maqtada Sadr led the fearsome Madhi Army in opposition to the US forces. During the course of the conflict, the Madhi Army engaged in ethnic cleansing in the Iraqi capital. John Hagan, Joshua Kaiser, Anna Hanson, Iraq and the Crimes of Aggressive War: The Legal Cynicism of Criminal Militarism (New York: Cambridge University Press, 2015), 127. After a cease-fire was negotiated with the U.S., al-Sadr had difficulty controlling the more extremist elements in his Army. In 2008, he announced that the Madhi Army would be reorganized into a social services organization committed to nonviolence.

Gina Chen, "Radical Iraq Cleric in Retreat: Sadr, Power Waning, Plans Moderate Course; Retaining Militia," *Wall Street Journal* (August 5, 2008). In April 2016, protesters under al-Sadr's leadership briefly occupied the Parliament buildings in the highly fortified Green Zone, leading to fears that the government would fall, but at al-Sadr's command demonstrators withdrew peacefully. Falih Hassan, Omar Al-Jawoshy, and Tim Arango, "Protesters Storm Bagdad's Green Zone to Denounce Corruption," *The New York Times* (April 20, 2016).

273 Chenoweth and Stephan, *Why Civil Resistance Works*, 94.

274 Ibid, 102-106; see also Ervand Abrahamian, "Mass Protests in the Iranian Revolution, 1977–79," in *Civil Resistance and Power Politics: The Experience of Nonviolent Action from Gandhi to the Present* (eds. Adam Roberts and Timothy Garton Ash) (New York: Oxford University Press, 2009), 162–78.

275 Ibid, 110.

276 Ibid, 117.

277 Ibid, 202.

278 Gene Burns, "Ideology, Culture, and Ambiguity: the Revolutionary Process in Iran," *Theory and Society* 25, no. 3 (1996), 349–388 (noting the "ambiguous ideology" of the Iranian revolution helped to unify the opposition).

279 In contrast, the Tunisian Ennadha party had internalized a culture of democracy and cooperation with other groups, prior to the fall of Ben Ali. Adam Roberts, "The Arab Spring: Why did things go so badly wrong?" *The Guardian* (January 15, 2016).

280 Whether this was in fact true is a matter of some controversy. Shadi Hami and Meredith Wheeler of the Brookings Institute evaluated Morsi's year in office according to a widely-used measure of autocracy and democracy, the Polity IV Index. They found that "Egypt under Morsi was undergoing a remarkably ordinary transition, neither wholly autocratic nor wholly democratic, falling almost exactly at the mean value of political transitions globally." "Opinion," Brookings (March 31, 2014), http://www.brookings.edu/research opinions/2014/03/31-egypt-morsi-autocrat-hamids. In contrast, the military government that came into power after the coup is even more repressive than most governments that have come to power after military coups, "bringing Egypt on par with Chile and Argentina in the 1970s and, more recently, Algeria in the 1990s; Ibid.

281 Stephen Zunes, "Civilian Defiance and Resistance to Coups and Military Takeovers," ICNC webinar (October 3, 2013), https://www.nonviolent-conflict.org/civilian-defiance-and-resistance-to-coups-and-military-takeovers/.

282 Kathryn Sikkink, *The Justice Cascade: How Human Rights Prosecutions Are Changing World Politics* (New York: W. W. Norton & Company, 2011), 33.

283 Sikkink, *The Justice Cascade*.

284 Transitional justice as an area of law is still quite unsettled, and there has been robust debate about the merits of trading "peace" for "justice." The following analysis takes no position on the question of whether the optimal form of accountability is criminal prosecution.

285 Though her focus is Latin America, Sikkink includes Greece and Portugal as important antecedents which "navigate[d] without a map" in prosecuting leaders of a former military junta in domestic courts.

286 Sikkink, *The Justice Cascade*, 44.

287 Ibid, 45.

288 Ibid.

289 Ibid, 46.

290 Naomi Roht-Arriaza, "State Responsibility to Investigate and Prosecute Grave Human Rights Violations in International Law," *California Law Review* 78, (1990), 449.

291 Previously perceived as a "gentleman's anti-communist club," the membership of the IACHR changed in the 1970s to include democrats and even those who had themselves been persecuted by repressive regimes. Sikkink, Justice Cascade, 64-65. The IACHR first called for prosecutions in a report on human rights violations in Chile in 1974 and 1977; and then again in reports on El Salvador and Haiti in 1979. Ibid, 67. The impact of the IACHR was enhanced after Jimmy Carter became US President in 1976, because he authorized funding for it which enabled it to do more effective in-country investigations. Ibid, 64.

292 Ibid.

293 Ibid.

294 Ibid, 69.

295 Naomi Roht-Arriaza, "Truth Commissions and Amnesties in Latin America: The Second Generation," *American Society of International Law Proceedings* 92 (1998), 313-14.

296 Manny Mogato, "Philippines invokes people power, 25 years on, to end corruption," *Reuters* (February 25, 2011), http://www.reuters.com/article/us-philippines-idUSTRE71O1YI20110225).

297 Shaazka Beyerle, "People Power versus Corruption," in *Is Authoritarianism Staging a Comeback?* (Atlantic Council, 2015).

[298] Carothers and Youngs, *The Complexities of Global Protests*, 8. Carothers and Youngs also observe, "In this broader sense, the emphasis on corruption in protests in many parts of the world reflects a general pattern of civic anger about how state power is exercised." Today's protest wave is in part a reflection of citizen fatigue with corruption, in part a legacy of the global financial crisis, and in part a widespread rejection of economic austerity." Ibid; 22.

[299] C. Raj Kumar, "Corruption and Human Rights: Promoting Transparency in Governance and the Fundamental Right to Corruption-Free Service in India," *Columbia Journal of Asian Law* 17 (2003), 51–52 (noting that "very little work [has been] done in examining the relationship of corruption to human rights and vice versa.")

[300] Kofi Annan, "Statement on the Adoption by the General Assembly of the United Nations Convention Against Corruption" (speech of the Secretary-General, New York, NY, October 31, 2003).

[301] Matthew Murray and Andrew Spalding, "Freedom from Official Corruption as a Human Right" (Washington: Governance Studies at Brookings (2015), 4.

[302] Matt Ellis, "Miller and Chevalier Releases Results of 2016 Latin America Corruption Survey," FCPAmericas Blog (August 8, 2016), 2016 WLNR 24131775. These results were consistent with earlier surveys done in 2008 and 2012.

[303] Murray and Spalding, "Freedom from Official Corruption as a Human Right," 4.

[304] Protesters march against corruption in Moldova.

[305] Murray and Spalding, "Freedom from Official Corruption as a Human Right," (noting "the major international instruments as well as academic and civil society commentators, generally regard corruption as merely a means of violating other, already-recognized human rights.")

[306] Andrew Brady Spalding, "The Irony of International Business Law: U.S. Progressivism and China's New Laissez-Faire," *University of California Los Angeles Law Review* 59 (2011), 355 (2011) (citing James R. Hines, Jr., Forbidden Payment: Foreign Bribery and American Business After 1977 (National Bureau of Economic Research, Working Paper No. 5266 (1995)), http://www.nber.org/papers/w5266. pdf). Hines's report focused on the US and the Foreign Corrupt Practices Act and was subject to a number of methodological criticisms; however, the basic findings were later confirmed by Alvaro Cuervo-Cazurra, "Who Cares About Corruption?," *Journal of International Business Studies* 37 (2006), 807 (finding that countries that ratified the Organisation for Economic Co-operation and Development (OECD) subsequently showed a marked decline in foreign direct investment in "more corrupt" countries).

[307] Ibid, 402 (citing Alvaro Cuervo-Cazurra, at 814).

[308] Andrew Brady Spalding, "Corruption, Corporations, and the New Human Right," *Washington University Law Review* 91 (2014), 1397.

[309] Ibid.

[310] Ibid, 1398.

[311] Personal communication from Andy Spalding.

[312] Interview with Jamel Betteib, July 2015.

[313] Lucas Barasa, "Ongeri protest activists released," *Daily Nation* (June 22, 2011), http://www.nation.co.ke/news/Onger -protest-activists-released/-/1056/1186954/-/a5rl45/-/index.html.

[314] "Anti-Corruption Protests Around the World – In Pictures," *The Guardian* (March 18, 2016), https://www.theguardian.com/global-development-professionals-network/gallery/2016/mar/18/anti-corruption-protests-around-the-world-in-pictures.

[315] UNKUT's efforts are directed against the post-2008 crash austerity economics imposed by the British government, like many other governments in Europe, which have drastically cut social services on which the less well-off in the UK depend.

[316] UK UNKUT is discussed in Peter Ackerman and Shaazka Beyerle, "Lessons from Civil Resistance for the Battle against Financial Corruption," *Sage Journals* 61, no. 3-4 (2014), https://www.nonviolent-conflict.org/lessons-from-civil-resistance-for-the-battle-against-financial-corruption.

[317] Shaazka Beyerle, *Curtailing Corruption: People Power for Accountability and Justice* (Boulder: Lynne Rienner Publishers, 2014), 39.

[318] Ibid, 42.

[319] Beyerle describes many more inventive nonviolent civil resistance tactics in ibid.

[320] Thomas M. Franck, "The Emerging Right to Democratic Governance," *American Journal of International Law* 86 (1992), 47–48. Franck's article does not speak to the question of non-state actors have a duty to help promote democracy as an international right.

[321] ICCPR, Art. 1(1).

[322] ICCPR, Art. 25 (a) and (b).

[323] Matthew Lister, "There is no Human Right to Democracy. But May We Promote It Anyway?" *Stanford Journal of International Law* 48 (2012), 257 (arguing that there is no right to democracy but democracy promotion may be good policy).

[324] For a more elaborated analysis of the "effective control" doctrine in international law and the role of a "dormant social contract," see Wilson, "'People Power' and the Problem of Sovereignty," 551-594.

[325] Ibid.

[326] James Crawford, "Right of Self-Determination in International Law," in Philip Alston, *People's Rights* (Oxford: Oxford University Press, 2001), 16 (noting references in Arts. 1 and 55 of the Charter were "somewhat ambiguous: what was the effect of the reference of self-determination in [these Articles], so far as non-colonial territories were concerned?")

[327] Ibid; see also ibid, 10 (noting "we have the paradox that the international law of self-determination both exists and is obscure.")

[328] Noting that many state parties did not address Art. 1 in their reports, the HRC stated that "States parties should describe the constitutional and political processes which in practice allow the exercise of this right." General Comment 12, Art. 1, para. 4, Compilation of General Comments and General Recommendations Adopted by Human Rights Treaty Bodies, U.N. Doc. HRI/GEN/1/Rev.1, 12 (1994).

[329] Ibid, para. 6.

[330] Ibid.

[331] Ibid, para. 4.

[332] See, e.g., Obiora Chinedu Okafor, *Legitimizing Human Rights NGO's: Lessons from Nigeria* (Trenton: Africa World Press, 2006), 8 ("NGO's were largely founded by elite, urbanized, Lagos-based civil rights lawyers (and other such professionals) who were…mostly focused on undermining military rule in Nigeria, and who marginalized too often other equally-important human rights issues…").

[333] Padraig McAuliffe, "The Roots of Transitional Accountabilities: Interrogating the 'Justice Cascade,'" *International Journal of Law in Context* 9 (2013), 106 (rev. of Sikkink, *The Justice Cascade* and Tricia Olsen, Leigh Payne and Andrew Reiter, *Transitional Justice In Balance: Comparing Processes, Weighing Efficacy*) (arguing that "what is seen as a justice cascade may in fact amount to merely an advocacy cascade, which has facilitated justice policies that democratizing states would inevitably have pursued"); see also Eric Posner, *Twilight of Human Rights* (Oxford: Oxford University Press, 2014), 26 ("The world is a freer place than it was 50 years ago, but is it freer because of the human rights or because of other events – such as economic growth or the collapse of communism?")

[334] Beth Simmons, *Mobilizing for Human Rights: International Law in Domestic Contexts* (Cambridge University Press, 2009), 159.

[335] Wilhelm G. Grewe, *The Epochs of International Law* (trans. Michael Byers) (New York: Walter de Gruyter, 2000), 7 (rejecting the "narrow view" where only "modern sovereign states" were subjects of international law and instead "considering the structural characteristics of an international legal order to be the essential criteria for examination").

[336] Anthony D'Amato, "Human Rights as Part of Customary International Law: A Plea for Change of Paradigms," *Georgia Journal of International and Comparative Law* 25 (1996), 71. D'Amato refers in passing to the "long and sorry history of reification of national entities: the bloody wars of nationalism in the 19th century (reviving today in Yugoslavia and parts of Africa), the deification of the State in Hegelian philosophy (laying a theoretical foundation for Hitler's Germany and the ensuing world war and holocaust), and the general degradation of the individual as nothing more than a servant of the state." But this is done only to frame the *reductio ad absurdum* argument that a "Human Rights Paradigm" as a corrective to the "Sovereignty Paradigm" would count only interpersonal, not inter-state, relations towards the formation of international law.

[337] Kofi Annan, *We the Peoples: the Role of the UN in the 21st Century* 48 (2000).

[338] Report of the International Commission on Intervention and State Sovereignty, *The Responsibility to Protect* (Ottowa: International Development Research Centre, 2001), para. 2.13.

[339] Wilson, "'People Power' and the Problem of Sovereignty," 576-77.

[340] Hardy Merriman, "Introduction to Civil Resistance", 2015 ICNC Summer Institute, https://www.nonviolent-conflict.org/introduction-to-civil-resistance/ (from part I, 14:24, and part II).

[341] Erica Chenoweth, "Online Methodological Index Accompanying 'Why Civil Resistance Works'" (2011), 3. http://www.du.edu/korbel/sie/media/documents/data/navco_1-1_appendix-and-codebook.pdf.

[342] General Assembly resolutions do not have the force of law; however, when they are adopted by consensus, as the DHRD was, they evince the *opinio juris* of the international community.

[343] Chenoweth and Stephan, *Why Civil Resistance Works*.

[344] See e.g., Shaazka Beyerle and Tina Olteanu, "How Romanian People Power Took on Mining and Corruption," *Foreign Policy* (November 17, 2016), http://foreignpolicy.com/2016/11/17/how-romanian-people-power-took-on-mining-and-corruption-rosia-montana/.

[345] A few ambiguous or contested entities, like Taiwan, Kosovo, and the Holy See, are not full United Nations members.

[346] "…as object, the individual is but a thing from the point of view of this law or that he is benefited or restrained by this law only insofar and to the extent that it makes it the right or the duty of states to protect his interests or to regulate his conduct." Christiana

Ochoa, "The Individual and Customary International Law Formation," (152), (quoting George Manner, "The Object Theory of the Individual in International Law", *American Journal of International Law* 46 (1952), 428-29.)

[347] This definition is very slightly adapted from the Restatement (Third) of Foreign Relations Law of the United States (1987), §101.

[348] "Statute of the International Court of Justice" Art. 38 (4). "Publicist" is an older term that means scholar, jurist, or commentator.

[349] Restatement (Third) of Foreign Relations Law, §102.

[350] This duty is expressed through the concept of due diligence.

[351] UDHR, Preamble, GA Res. 217A (III), U.N. Doc. A/810 at 71 (1948).

[352] ICCPR, December 16, 1966, S. Exec. Rep. 102-23, 999 U.N.T.S. 171.

[353] ICESCR, December 16, 1966, S. Treaty Doc. No. 95-19, 6 I.L.M. 360 (1967), 993 U.N.T.S. 3.

[354] The new UNHRC was formed after a predecessor body called the Human Rights Commission was dissolved because of being widely perceived as illegitimate, in that major human rights abusing could win a seat on the Council and thereby block action against human-rights abusing countries. GA Res. 60/251 created the Human Rights Council.

[355] The European Commission is now defunct.